Giving Back:

Will you join us in giving back? One hundred percent of all profits generated by Contrarian Marketing books and DVDs are donated to my favorite organization, the Folds of Honor Foundation.

Folds of Honor provides post-secondary educational scholarships to the spouses and children of service members disabled or killed as a result of their military service to our great nation.

Today's servicemen and women bear the incredible burden of combat and face the same economic strain faced by the rest of the country. Folds of Honor recognizes the federal government's work to support its military service families, but it cannot succeed alone without proactive civilian organizations to assist.

Photo courtesy of Volvo Rents.

ALL GAVE SOME.
SOME GAVE ALL.
NOW IT'S OUR
TURN TO GIVE.

To learn more about the Folds of Honor Foundation, visit www.foldsofhonor.org.

This book is dedicated to my Mother who always lovingly taught me to press on.
– Nick

Con•trar•i•an

Noun:

A person who typically acts or thinks in a way contrary
to popular, accepted opinion or prevailing wisdom

Merriam-Webster Dictionary

TABLE OF CONTENTS

TABLE OF CONTENTS

ACKNOWLEDGMENT

It is an interesting process to reflect on how one collects knowledge.

Countless customers, colleagues, mentors, institutions, great newspapers and magazines have been my teachers for the last twenty years. They taught me Contrarian Marketing.

Don O'Neal taught me to 'take care of the customer'. John Moller taught me to look for 'an edge'.

My most treasured teacher has been the *Wall Street Journal*. Over a cup of coffee or lunch, the Journal distilled complex insights into nuggets of intelligence on how the best businesses succeed.

I am indebted to Barry Natwick, Chief Operating Officer of Volvo Rents, who provided the vision and support to focus the company on "Best of Best" customers, and allow my colleagues and me the latitude to engineer a superior customer experience.

A special note of gratitude to the team who assisted me:

Marie Bartlett, my editor, improved the original manuscript by at least 1,000 percent. Jan and Jim Franke, professional trainers, patiently reviewed the book and gave feedback about how to simplify the **Contrarian Marketing** methodology for a training environment.

Ken Myers, Janet Desloges and Alex Benizzi, my graphics team, transformed the **Contrarian Marketing** book, presentation and videos into a visual experience.

I am very grateful to my mentor, Ronald Goodstein, Ph.D., Professor of Marketing at Georgetown University's McDonough School of Business, who taught me the essence of marketing knowledge and who's insights have been vital to this book and to me through the years. There are only few leaders that I have met through my life who are able to casually convey a lifetime of marketing and business wisdom into a short presentation or conversation. Ron is one such person and a cherished friend.

And finally, to my mother, Katherine Ziegler, who lovingly nudged me to press on.

Nick Mavrick
Washington, D.C.
July, 2011

FOREWORD

> *"Give a man a fish; you have fed him for today.*
> *Teach a man to fish; and you have fed him for a lifetime."*
>
> —*Author Unknown*

My name is Major Dan Rooney and I am an F-16 fighter pilot in the Oklahoma National Guard who served three tours in Iraq. While I've seen the devastation of war from the cockpit, I had never witnessed its intimate side until returning home on a flight that carried the remains of a fallen solider. As the plane landed and the flag-covered casket was removed, the soldier's young son stood clutching his mother's leg. Passengers disembarked, some ignoring the pilot's request to remain seated as a sign of respect. At that point, I knew I had a new mission in life. Though I could not change the fate of a fallen comrade, I could help a grieving widow or a fatherless child.

That was the start of Folds of Honor, a nonprofit organization I founded in 2007 that offers healing and hope to families of killed or disabled veterans through scholarships and other assistance. Since education is the key to a better future I made it the basis for Folds of Honor by giving qualifying spouses and children a chance to pursue a postsecondary education of their choice. About 85 percent of these families do not qualify for VA educational benefits.

But I have not fulfilled this mission alone.

People like Nick Mavrick, author of **Contrarian Marketing**, have reached out to join me and many others in our quest to provide a brighter future for military personnel who made the ultimate sacrifice. Since our inception we have awarded more than 2400 scholarships and other aid worth an estimated ten million. Today, our work continues.

I met Nick in 2011 when he came to Oklahoma on behalf of Volvo Rents, another partner in our growing nonprofit. We shared a stage on Fox TV News that helped promote Folds of Honor. In the following weeks, Nick informed me that he was donating all proceeds from his book **Contrarian Marketing** to our 501c3 charitable organization. Nick is another example of the generosity and willingness of people across this great country reaching out to help those who fight and die for our personal freedoms.

While our servicemen and women continue to bear the burden of combat, we recognize that Folds of Honor contributions must continue as well. Please join me, Nick and others in our ongoing mission to salute our military veterans and their families in need.

My special thanks to Nick Mavrick with my best wishes to him and the success of *Contrarian Marketing.*

Major Dan Rooney
Founder, Folds of Honor Foundation
Owasso, Oklahoma
July 2011

CONTRARIAN MARK**E**TING

INTRODUCTION

While still a powerful engine of productivity,
the U.S. economy took a major hit in the last decade, and so did many businesses.

Introduction

> *"I don't look to jump over seven-foot bars:*
> *I look around for one-foot bars that I can step over."*
>
> —*Warren Buffett, investor*

Big trouble: That's how we ended the first decade of the 21st century, most economists agree. Housing bubbles out of control, risky investments, over-the-top customer spending, huge indebtedness, high unemployment, and mismanagement of the macro economy by those who should have known better. The list goes on and so does the end result: a severe recession from which, in 2011, we are still struggling to recover. This book will help prepare you for more economic instability ahead.

My name is Nick Mavrick and I believe that being a contrarian, someone who takes a different path, is a smart move in business today. As a Vice President of Marketing for a large multi-national company, I've conducted thousands of successful marketing campaigns and witnessed many in which companies set out to satisfy a wide range of customers that decide to try their services, buy their products, or simply walk through the door. Many of these tried-and-true marketing practices no longer work in managing customer relationships.

Big trouble: That's how we ended the first decade of the 21st century. Contrarian Marketing will help prepare you for more economic instability ahead. - Nick Mavrick

While still a powerful engine of productivity, the U.S. economy took a major hit in the last decade, and so did many businesses. Some survived. Some did not. All were impacted, good or bad, which leads to some important marketing questions:

In your business, would you market differently if you knew how much revenue and profits were created by the top ten, or 20 percent, of your customers? What if you learned that five percent of your customers generated over 70 percent of your revenue & profits? Or that your top customers' life-time value was five times or ten times larger than that of your average customer? Would you become a "contrarian" marketer if going against the grain would help you survive a dangerous world economy?

A few have already dared to be different and better. Among them were Harrah's Entertainment, Inc., the world's largest gaming company with about 50 casinos and more than 80,000 employees throughout the U.S. and the United Kingdom; Best Buy, the largest customer electronics outlet in the U.S. with a loyalty program that broke the norms with its "angel-demon"

plan; Burger King, designated number two in the fast food industry just behind McDonald's; Starwood Hotels (better known as Westin) with 980 properties in 100 countries; and Apple Computers, expert in drawing a younger crowd while maintaining customer loyalty among its most seasoned users. How did these firms excel relative to their competitors? The answer is that they went against the traditions in their industries to better accommodate customers and grow the profitability of their most loyal clientele.

Middle-income households made less in 2009, adjusted for inflation, than they did in 1999.

I am convinced that picking your customers before they pick you is more important than ever in a global market in which economic experts predict and/ or acknowledge the following:

- The U.S. borrowed more from China than it had been buying in 2010. As of April 2011 China held $1.2 tillion of U.S. debt.

- We have a decline in American economic power according to World Bank president Robert Zoellick.

- Over the next decade, additional government deficits will top nine trillion dollars and anticipated growth will not cover this bill.

- There has been zero net job creation since 1999. In addition, economic output rose at its slowest rate of any decade since the 1930s.

- Middle-income households made less in 2010, when adjusted for inflation, than they did in 1999.

- Total household debt rose 114 percent from 1999 to its peak in 2008 according to Federal Reserve data, leading some economists to reference this ongoing period as "the lost decade."

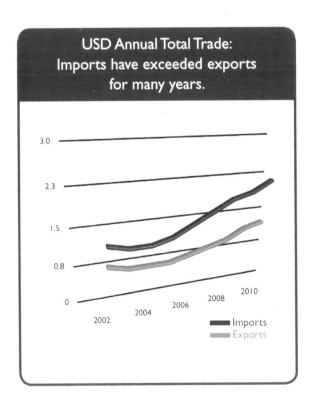

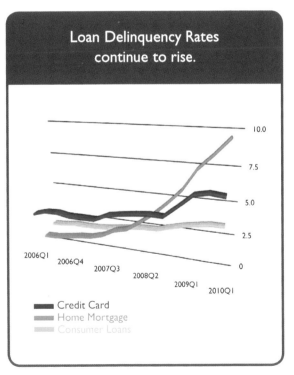

- More Americans filed for bankruptcy protection in July, 2010, reversing a trend of declining filings over the previous three months. (*Wall Street Journal*, "Personal Bankruptcies Rise, Reversing Trend" 08/05/2010).

- In June, 2010 pending home sales plunged to their lowest level since 2001.

- Spending was flat as Americans continued to grapple with high unemployment. Some rebounding has occured in 2011.

Today, experts on the left think the economy won't expand without more government control, while those on the right say too much government control has made business leaders afraid to take risks. Yet business can survive, reinvent itself; even thrive.

But none of this will happen without a new approach, one that recognizes that if you are to control your businesses' destinies, then you must concentrate on VIP customers by picking the "*Best of Best*" (hereafter in the book referred to as B-of-B).

Marketing is a science first; an art second. Therefore, your approach should be rooted in fact-based decision making.

It was a perfect storm for many businesses, like Circuit City, who closed all stores in 2009.

Contrarian Marketing is a maverick methodology that enables you to execute a clear, quantifiable and focused marketing strategy—one that allows you to target the five to ten percent of your B-of-B customers and prospects who drive the majority of your revenue and profits.

Its premise is that you can pick your customers before they pick you, aiming your break-through marketing capital and campaigns at VIP customers. You can facilitate gain and expedite your competitor's loss by focusing on B-of-B customers and future B-of-B customers. On balance, the U.S. economy remains a powerful engine of productivity, and some say growth will come despite major challenges including health care, climate change, and government regulation. But no one really knows what's ahead.

That's why **Contrarian Marketing** is the right methodology at the right time. **Contrarian Marketing** will improve your business success no matter which future predictions prove correct. Simply put, this text is a guide through uncertain economic times to carefully choosing your best clients or, more precisely, quantitative marketing as opposed to the "one size fits all" approach. We've seen this approach too often in the past, and will continue to see it unless business understands that the world has changed, and if they are to adapt, they must change their marketing approach along with it.

Consider this:

- According to a 2008 yearlong study of more than 1300 brands and 54 million shoppers by Catalina Marketing, 1.2 percent of shoppers accounted for 80 percent of Budweiser's sales; only one percent of Iams pet food customers accounted for a whopping 80 percent of their volume, and only 2.5 percent of customers accounted for 80 percent of sales of the average package-goods brand. Virtually all brands studied generated 80 percent of sales from 10 percent or less of shoppers.

Contrarian Marketing will improve your business success no matter which predictions of the future prove correct.

- At Volvo Rents, an international construction equipment rental company, ten percent of customers generate 83 percent of revenue and profits; and transact 12+ times per year. We call this group B-of-B customers. The company allocates 80 percent of its marketing capital to marketing to the top ten percent of customers and prospects.

> **Marketing is a science first; an art second.**

• Burger King provides another example: 25 percent of customers generate 50 percent of revenue and transact over 15 times per month. Burger King used this data to guide its future menu to cater to its best customers. They added a one-pound breakfast burrito to broaden their appeal to their B-of-B clients.

• As early as 2004 Best Buy 'fired' their lowest tier customers in exchange for greater focus on large spenders. According to the *Wall Street Journal* the big box retailer decided not all customers were welcome. Reward Zone members accounted for only about 30 percent of their transactions, but spent $844 a year compared to about $400 for other customers.

• Harrah's Entertainment identified a small group of customers who produced most of the company's profits. They found that people who spent between $100 and $499 per trip accounted for about 30 percent of gamblers, but were 80 percent of revenue and nearly 100 percent of profits.

• Starwood Hotels (Westin) took customer segmentation to a new level with a "secret" pilot program to target only the prime customers of competitive hotels. More on that later.

• According to the National Golf Foundation, avid golfers (those who play 25 or more rounds a year) constitute 23 percent of all players and generate 63 percent of spending on fees and equipment.

Not all customers are created equal, at least in terms of their loyalty, and therefore profitability.

Harrah's found that 30% of gamblers represented 80% of revenue/100% of profit.

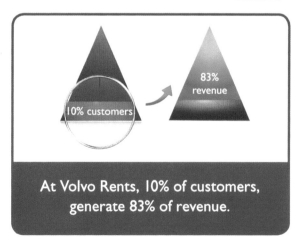

83% revenue

10% customers

At Volvo Rents, 10% of customers, generate 83% of revenue.

- If you don't think customers are picking you before you pick them, then consider this: the distinction between shopping online (e-tail) and in-store (retail) is fast disappearing, according to chief executive of The Find, which collects more than 400 million product listings from Web sites and stores. The conclusion drawn was that in-store retailers must match their online competitors' prices or the customer will *walk out of the store.*

Though **Contrarian Marketing** goes far beyond the tried-and-true "80/20" principle and gives you a nuts-and-bolts business model presented in detail, there is still merit in the basic 80/20 premise. The premise is credited to Vilfredo Pareto, a 19th century economist, who noted that 80% of the wealth in a society is usually attributed to 20% of the population. J.M. Juran noted that this same principle held across many other types of relationships in society and business. He coined the term the Pareto Principle, which later became known as the Rule of 80/20 (Robert Sanders (1988), "The Pareto Principle: Its Use and Abuse," *The Journal of Business & Industrial Marketing,* 3 (2), 37- 40.). The author of The *80/20 Principle,* Richard Koch, says "markets and customers, on which any firm should be centered, must be the *right* ones, typically a small minority of those that the company currently owns." He goes on to state the three "golden rules" of effective, <u>segmented</u> marketing:

The "Golden Rules" of Effective, Segmented Marketing

Golden Rule #1:

Focus on providing a stunning product and exceptional service in 20 percent of the existing product line, for it will generate 80 percent of your fully-costed profits.

Golden Rule #2:

Your marketing should devote time and efforts toward delighting and keeping forever those 20 percent of customers who provide 80 percent of sales and profits.

Golden Rule #3:

All innovation is product-led. Since you are likely to obtain more than 80 percent of your true profits from 20 percent of your product line, focus your creative marketing on new products or services within that 20 percent, particularly if the product/service/price/packaging is obtainable elsewhere. Your only hope to compete is to innovate, and you can't innovate without a new product or service.

Source: Richard Koch, author of, *The 80/20 Principle*

Want to feel how close "failure" is to your own business? On your next drive down a major street in your city count the empty spaces in the strip malls and shopping centers, or consider all the restaurants at which you frequently dined, that are now closed.

Innovative firms that failed the Contrarian Marketing test.

In marketing, many of us have been taught to be followers—blissfully imitating what our competitors do, and wondering why sub-par profitability plagues many industries and companies.

A competitor's marketing campaign or strategy, especially if implemented by the market leader, has a curious seduction on the followers. I can hear middle management within these companies as they plead with their bosses: "Let's do what they do, and we'll become the market leader."

But if you follow this line of logic, you may end up like competitors we all know—AIG, General Motors, and 120 banks in the first few months of 2010, many of which are out of business or became dependent upon government assistance to survive.

Want to feel how close "failure" is to your own business? On your next drive down a major street in your city, count the empty spaces in the strip malls and shopping centers, or consider all the restaurants, at which you frequently dined, that are now closed.

Now personalize some of these failures to your own industry. Think of a few competitors or businesses that are struggling today. Maybe they've already failed and their doors are closed. It's likely that even some of your customers are no longer around. Not good signs.

All you have to do is dare to be different: that is *"be a contrarian"* in your marketing by following the guidelines presented here. You will be better than your competitors as a result.

> *Retaining an additional 2 percent of customers has the same effect*
> *as cutting costs 10 percent.*
> *—Davidow & Malone, the Virtual Corporation*

The central premises of *Contrarian Marketing* are five-fold:

1. **"Best of the Best" customers (VIPs, repeat customers or 'regulars') generate the majority of most businesses revenue and profit.** They account for a small percentage of total customers and a large percentage of revenue and profit. For many companies, ten percent of customers generate 70 percent of revenue and profits.

2. **Customize Your Customer Support Systems to Support the "Best of the Best" customers exclusively.** Given the importance of B-of-B customers, it is essential that you tailor your operations and your entire company so that these customers have complete flexibility and adapt processes that support them.

3. **Clone your "Best of the Best" customers.** Instead of focusing on busy work and marketing to the masses, your central aim should be focused on multiplying your success with B-of-B customers by identifying their behaviors and characteristics, and cloning them into B-of-B prospects.

4. **Stay true to the Yearly and Lifetime Value of Customers.** By focusing on the yearly and lifetime profitability of your customers, you can shift out of short-term decision making, and instead evaluate their profitability to your business over a longer period of time. You can then tailor your business support processes to the different segments within your customer base (specifically B-of-B customers). Many businesses treat all customers the same—or resort to 'lowest common denominator decision making: "If I make an exception for you, then I will need to make exceptions for everyone." Yearly and lifetime value calculations wiill allow your employees to make exceptions for your B-of-B customers.

5. **Develop an Early Warning System for "Recently Departed" Customers.** Develop an enterprise-wide early warning system that lets you know when a B-of-B customer defects or can no longer maintain his or her status as one of your best customers. An early warning system allows you to quickly respond to a competitor poaching your B-of-B customers or a customer service issue. Timely action is essential to keeping these valuable customers.

Make a choice, consciously, as to how you will market—either choose to market to the masses or choose to market to only a few. Will you spread your efforts across the board or concentrate your efforts on the few customers and prospects that drive the majority of your revenue and profits?

The **Contrarian Marketing** methodology is effective for any type of business-to-business enterprise. Whether you run a large company or small, a division, a district, a field office, or work as a sales person, it is designed for you. If you are in Finance, Healthcare, Information Technology, Consulting, Manufacturing, Politics or Law, to name a few, it will serve as an invaluable guide to help focus your marketing initiatives.

In summary, what will you get from this book? You will gain the knowledge and the tools to achieve clarity in how you should market to your core customers. Specifically, you will know how to craft a simple marketing plan that will enable you and your sales team to act with confidence and get a *quantifiable* return out of your marketing efforts aimed at the right customers.

If you pay attention to your customer data, the data will take the mystery out of marketing and let you market smarter and more efficiently with your precious marketing capital.

It's the equivalent of counting cards in Blackjack and doubling your bets when you are dealt a favorable hand. The result: winning at an accelerated rate by concentrating on the outcomes with the highest probabilities of winning. And we all want to win, don't we?

In the well-received book *Bringing Down the House: The Inside Story of Six M.I.T. Students Who Took Vegas for Millions* (the movie "21" starring Kevin Spacey was based upon this book), one of the main characters had just placed a highly successful bet. When asked how the (bleep) he had pulled it off, he replied:

> *"It's not magic; just math. It's called shuffle tracking. It's a basic probability-distribution exercise. You can even calculate the percentage of low-card infiltration into the run, caused by a dealer's shuffle. After that, it's just a matter of practice. Really good players can track a group of fifteen cards through a six-deck shuffle without breaking a sweat."*

> ### It's not magic; just math.

That's what **Contrarian Marketing** provides: a quantifiable approach using the "right" numbers to reach logical conclusions about your targeted customers. In the first chapter you'll see exactly how to go about finding those numbers, and where to place your most successful bet; one that is not magic, just math.

CONTRARIAN
MARKΞTING

CHAPTER ONE:
QUANTITATIVE MARKETING, CONTRARIAN STYLE

Chapter One: Quantitative Marketing, Contrarian Style

> *"Wide diversification is only required*
> *when investors do not understand what they are doing."*
>
> —*Warren Buffett, investor*

From the CEO's suite to field salespersons, marketing is often thought of as whatever the latest advertising campaign happens to be. Input to the marketing department is alarmingly subjective—determining the marketing budget, writing advertising copy, modifying the tone of a marketing campaign or changing the color of a logo are too often what drives the campaign.

Marketers are to blame for this, as B2B marketing folks are often clueless about the results they hope to achieve. As a marketer, I've made some of these same mistakes myself. Marketing in the B2B environment is established to make the sales person's job easier. To do so, the marketing and sales force must come together as a team. That is the best way to assure consistent and relevant messaging and delivery, and more impactful results. This is a simple idea, but appears contrarian to the way so many B2B companies work.

Today, with data, facts, information, and knowledge serving a more important function than ever before, it takes a measurable and analytical approach to buyer behaviors to maximize marketing investments. Those marketers who focus on the top five percent—the B-of-B customers and the prospects that generate 70 percent or more of revenue and profits, will earn the trust of the CEO suite and the field by demonstrating *quantifiable* returns.

As a central member of a customer-focused team, sales people with direct customer contact will find the **Contrarian Marketing** principles and methods helpful in recruiting and closing more of the right contracts that lead to long-term profitability. Begin to think of your sales efforts as fact-based decision-making, with extreme focus on B-of-B customers utilizing high-impact marketing techniques.

In this chapter, we will show you how other companies made marketing quantitative and therefore more cost-effective without losing the power of building a relationship. You'll learn the importance of 'picking your customers before they pick you'. Moreover, you will learn the quantitative significance of acquiring your competitors' top customers—and how that achievement alone can propel your success and accelerate your competitors' demise.

I like to acquire my competitors one customer at a time.
—Michael Dell

Courtesy of Dell Inc.

What Relationship Marketing Does:
• Focuses on profitable retention
• Emphasizes customer value
• Provides longer-term time scale
• Allows high customer service emphasis
• Is concerned with relationship quality

—Ronald C. Goodstein, Ph.D.

Michael Dell, of Dell Computer, summed it up best: "I like to acquire my competitors one customer at a time."

First, whether in management or sales, make a conscious decision as to how you will market—choosing either to market to the masses or to only a few. Will you spread your time, energy, and resources across the board or concentrate on the few customers and prospects that drive the majority of your revenue and profits?

Before you answer that question, let's find out what others think and have done.

Once a student leader of the Chinese Tiananmen Square protests, Li Lu is now a hedge-fund manager and in line to become a successor to Warren Buffett at Berkshire Hathaway, Inc. He told investors he has learned a valuable lesson on segmentation. Watching the World Cup, he compared his investment style to soccer.

"You may very well work hard and seldom score," he said. "But occasionally you get one or two great chances. That's when you make decisive strikes that really matter" (*Wall Street Journal*, "From Tiananmen Square to Possible Buffett Successor." 07/30/10).

Dr. Ronald C. Goodstein, Ph.D., at Georgetown University's McDonough School of Business, maintains that contemporary relationship marketing includes combining several marketing techniques in order to create a stronger business model. It's called **customer portfolio management, which is a process of having**

dedicated marketing teams assigned to best customers, next-best customers, etc. and allocating marketing capital proportionately.

Relationships with your B-of-B customers are a source of competitive advantage, Dr. Goodstein says. But companies must know through their client relationships how to choose the *right* customers.

"We can no longer churn through customers, assuming there will always be another one," he said. "Neither can we serve them in the old ways. Their expectations are higher and their commitment weaker. Since some customers will cost you money, convert them to profitability or lose them. **Think like an investor: buy a customer today, get returns tomorrow. But first, know how to find the right ones."**

The following case study exemplifies the method and merits of determining how many customers you really need—a basic concept of *Contrarian Marketing*.

Case Study #1: World's Largest Gaming Company Hits the Jackpot with New Strategy

Harrah's became the world's top gaming company when it acquired Caesars Entertainment for $9.4 billion in 2005. Operations now include casino hotels, dockside and floating casinos, and Native American gaming facilities spread over some three million square feet throughout the U.S. and the U.K. Much of their success is attributed to a strategy that involved identifying their best customers and treating them as well as they did high rollers.

At the center of this strategy was Gary W. Loveman, a former Harvard professor who began as a consultant to Harrah's and then became its CEO. Loveman applied a vast mathematical model similar to the ones economists use to predict the gross national product.

Before long, avid experienced players became Harrah's target customers.

The mathematical method Loveman advocated scored gamblers on their profitability to the casino. It was referred to as "Pavolovian Marketing," followed by sizing up gamblers "psycho-graphically," or rating them according to characteristics such as their careers and lifestyles. Thus, a small group of Harrah's customers were identified who produced most of the company's profits. Specifically, it was determined that *while people who spent between $100 and $499 a trip accounted for only about 30 percent of gamblers, they accounted for 80 percent of revenue and surprisingly nearly 100 percent of profits.*

Professor Loveman found that a lack of customer loyalty was Harrah's biggest weakness. Noting that clients spent only 36 cents of every wagering dollar at Harrah's, he realized that if the company could raise that amount by one penny, annual earnings would jump by more than $1 a share.

As a result of his findings, Loveman designed targeted marketing strategies to appeal to this segment. The bottom line was that Harrah's market share increased around the country. Revenues rose at nearly double the rate of nearby casinos after the new targeted marketing was introduced. In addition, customers' discretionary spending with Harrah's rose: up from 30 to nearly 50 percent more compared to Harrah's competitors.

Harrah's now clearly identifies their 'best' customers, and treats them as VIPs. Their

Harrah's determined that while people who spent $100 and $499 a trip accounted for only about 30 percent of gamblers, they accounted for 80 percent of revenue and surprisingly nearly 100 percent of profits.

innovative marketing techniques and sophisticated data bases are currently considered one of the most advanced customer relationship management systems in the industry. This allows them to customize predictions for their regional markets as well.

"Without this system," concluded Chief Marketing Officer David Morton, "Harrah's would have to send blanket marketing materials to everyone on its mailing list, lowering profitability of marketing campaigns (Source: http://gaming.univ.edu).

Case Study #2: **Best Buy Separates the Angels from the Demons**

Best Buy Company operates more than 1400 stores throughout the U.S. and Canada and another 2600 stores in Europe and China. Despite the economic climate that has diminished or eliminated major retailers in the past decade, its share of the electronics market has risen nearly every year since 2000 when it claimed 15 percent of the market. In 2008, it was named second among the world's six "most admired specialty retailers" (*Fortune*, "World's Most Admired Companies," March 16, 2009, pg 86).

At the Minneapolis headquarters of Best Buy, the company installed a mock "retail hospital," that included a row of fallen retailers in bed (their logos propped on pillows) including the old Woolworth five-and-dime. A sign nearby stated: '*This is Where Companies Go When Their Strategies Get Sick*'. The point was to keep Best Buy out of those hospital beds and ahead of the big healthy guys: Wal-Mart and Costco.

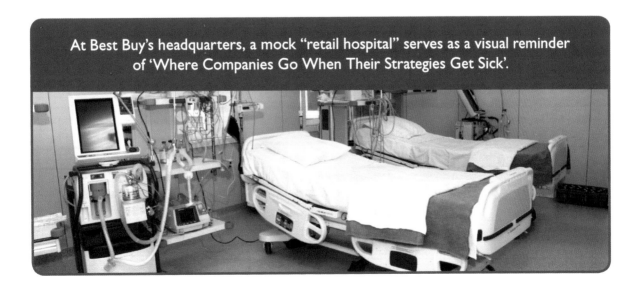

At Best Buy's headquarters, a mock "retail hospital" serves as a visual reminder of 'Where Companies Go When Their Strategies Get Sick'.

The mock hospital is also a visual reminder that in the volatile world of low-margin retailing, complacency and follower strategies can spell illness, even death.

CEO Brad Anderson, known for producing research that tied a company's stock-market value to its ability to identify and cater to profitable customers, decided to hire a consultant. His name was Larry Selden, professor of Finance and Economics at Columbia University's Graduate School of Business, and co-author (along with *Fortune's* Geoffrey Colvin) of *Angel Customers and Demon Customers* (Portfolio, 2003). Professor Selden argued that at many companies, losses produced by devil customers wiped out profits generated by angels. He insisted that a company should view itself as a portfolio of customers, not product lines.

Anderson liked the idea of separating the "angels" among his 1.5 million daily customers from the "demons." Within the inner workings of Best Buy, the new approach became known as "centricity." Basically, it means figuring out which customers make you the most money, segmenting them carefully, realigning your business, and training your employees to *target favored shoppers with products and services that motivate them to return again and again.* **Contrarian Marketing applies this same process to B2B.**

Purchasing histories of several groups of customers were analyzed, with an eye toward identifying bad customers who purchased loss-leading merchandise and returned purchases. As a result, **the group discovered it could distinguish the angels from the devils, and that 20 percent of Best Buy's customers accounted for the bulk of profits.**

"It's really about saying you have a limited pool of money, and as a business person you need to spend that money where you can get the most return," explained Kelly Hlavinka, of Frequency Marketing, the ad agency that created Best Buy's Reward Zone loyalty program (*Fortune Magazine*, "Best Buy's Giant Gamble," No. 6, 2006).

While Best Buy has benefited from the liquidation of Circuit City, the deep recession that led to its rival's elimination also hurt Best Buy's financial results, leading to a steep drop in net income in 2008. Former CEO Brad Anderson said that "seismic" changes in consumer behavior have created "the most difficult climate" ever seen by the retailer. However, business bounced back in the latest fiscal year with revenue up more than 10% and profitability on the rise, although modestly. With Circuit City out of the picture, Best Buy still faces stiff competition from Amazon. com, which has experienced rapid growth in consumer electronics sales, low-price leader Wal-Mart Stores, and Costco Wholesale, among many others. Indeed, in response to the changing competitive landscape and increased online shopping by consumers, Best Buy has announced plans to double its $2 billion in online sales within three to five years and is shrinking the size of some of its vast stores (Hoover's).

Best Buy understood if they were going to succeed, change must follow.

Case Study #3: Starwood Hotels (Westin) Launches Secret Program to Acquire Best Customers

One of the world's largest hotel and leisure companies, Starwood Hotels & Resorts Worldwide, counts among its holding nearly 1,000 properties across the globe. It began in 1995 from a nearly bankrupt real estate investment trust and grew into one of the world's largest hotel companies with a value exceeding $14 billion (*Sales & Marketing Mgt.* #158, "A Transformative Experience, 2006).

Starwood took customer segmentation to a new level with a "secret" pilot program launched in late 2009; one that explored new ways to identify prime customers based on factors other than frequency of stay, the key measure in traditional hotel loyalty programs. Guests' earning potential and their ability to influence other travelers was also measured.

It was "secret" in that the hotel chain took great pains to keep the details under wraps despite inviting thousands of customers to participate. There was even a code name for the pilot project, which was separate from Starwood Preferred Guest, the company's primary loyalty program for frequent guests, and the Ambassador program offered to select customers in 2008.

More unique, they targeted travelers loyal not only to Starwood but to competitive hotels. In addition to gathering data, the focus was one-on-one relationships between the customer and a designated Starwood ambassador, whose job it was to make their Starwood experience memorable by determining what mattered to each guest and how to make their stay even better. From the moment a guest came through the door, the hotel staff knew how to make him or her comfortable, whether through offering up herbal drinks and scented candles or providing access to a local fashion show. Celebrity-level chefs and "heavenly soft" beds

Starwood took customer segmentation to a new level with a "secret" pilot program launched in late 2009; one that explored new ways to identify prime customers based on factors other than frequency of stay, the key measure in traditional hotel loyalty programs.

> **It's a contrarian move, one that can translate to increased revenue.**

helped increase each experience and in the process enhanced customer loyalty.

In other words, Starwood made special efforts to offer individualized, personalized service: service that guests ultimately must have determined made a difference. As of 2010 Starwood is expanding the pilot. They are inviting more overseas travelers and exploring "breakthrough" ways to discover and engage new, high-value customers, as well as new ways to benefit existing guests (*USA Today*, March 11, 2010).

"We're reinventing the hotel experience," said CEO Steve Hayer in 2006. "There are different needs for different types of travel, and it's not just about price and location. Our bet is that it is all about experience".

It is also about quantitative marketing—looking at factors beyond how often guests stay and evaluating their lifetime growth potential in order to rebrand what is basically a commodity (a hotel room). **It's a contrarian move, one that can translate to increased revenue.**

It's similar to what happens in a card game. Splitting tens is sometimes a stupid move, says author Ben Mezrich in *Bringing Down the House*. But if the count is high and the dealer's card low, then it can also be extremely profitable.

"It's not luck; it's not gambling. It is the odds of winning, odds that are significantly higher than fifty-fifty" (Excerpt, page 83).

Now that you've learned a little about what quantitative marketing is, and how it is applied through case studies, let's look at the importance of understanding your own company's greatest assets—and how they can be put to best use.

Splitting tens is regarded by many to be a stupid move. However, if the count is high and the dealers card low, then it can be very profitable.

CONTRARIAN
MARK⅃TING

CHAPTER TWO:
FIRST, UNDERSTAND YOUR STRENGTHS

Chapter Two: First, Understand Your Strengths

> *"Victory does not come to those that play by the rules."*
>
> —*Genghis Khan*

In the 1990s, the most fearsome and revered boxer in the world was Mike Tyson—a World Champion for many years. A kid from the streets, molded and mentored by the great Cus D'Amato, the media followed him with intense interest. With strength and precision, he dominated and decimated opponent after opponent.

On February 11, 1990, something strange and unexpected happened. An unknown challenger defeated the great, unconquerable champion. Buster Douglas, a 42-1 challenger, brought down the house and Mike Tyson was never the same.

George Foreman, the former world champion of boxing had memorable remarks and profound advice for Mike Tyson after his loss to Douglas. In George's opinion, Mike Tyson was like a Ferrari – the greatest sports car the world had ever known. Except that Mike did not know what made him great because his success and skills came so effortlessly. His confidence and natural talent made him a champion. When Tyson lost the fight to Douglas—the equivalent of his Ferrari breaking down on the side of the road—Foreman related that Tyson did not know what he was, what he stood for, or what had previously made him unconquerable. In Tyson's mind, he had always been a champion.

Foreman related that Tyson did not know what he was, what he stood for, or what had previously made him unconquerable.

So when Tyson—using Foreman's car metaphor—walked to the front of the Ferrari—and opened the hood to find out what was wrong, instead of seeing a powerful engine, Tyson saw a skinny-legged chicken that pedaled the car to supersonic speeds.

It was a powerful visual that captured Foreman's advice to Tyson: since you have always been a champion, and now you are dethroned—go back to the basics. Understand what you are good at—even if it is a mirror of your past accomplishments. Appreciate your strengths and recognize them.

> *To excel consistently, it is essential that you understand why you are succeeding or failing. Once you understand your customer base, you can determine where you want to go.*

What happened and what is this story's relevancy to marketing? Marketing is not much different than boxing or any other sport. To excel consistently, it is essential that you understand why you are succeeding or failing. Once you understand your customer base, you can determine where you want to go.

Before we go any further, I want to introduce several concepts that I will be covering in this chapter and remaining parts of the book. This "Bill of Rights" will keep you focused on the key concepts as you read further:

A good example of bottom-up decision making is the Ritz Carlton that empowers its employees with the discretion to spend $2,000 on a customer to uphold the company's reputation for superior customer service.

It is easier to get current customers to do more, than it is to procure a new one.
—*Ronald C. Goodstein, Ph.D., Georgetown University*

Contrarian Marketing Bill of Rights

1. **Marketing success can be engineered by mathematically tying your company's business & financial objectives to acquisition and retention of your B-of-B "raving fan" customers.** Customer data and their percentage contribution to your company's revenue and profitability allows you to establish a neutral framework in which you can engage participation from your employees centered around data. Your marketing strategy is now 'data-centered' or *quantitative*, as opposed to focusing on the opinion-based, subjective *qualitative* side of marketing (advertising design, colors of logos, etc.—the proverbial "tail wagging the dog").

   By analyzing your company's financial plan (revenue & profits) you can successfully create a simple table that details the number of customers and prospects that drive the majority of your revenue & profits. This table will focus the marketing program on customer segmentation, the ten percent/70 percent rule and the proportional allocation of marketing capital to your B-of-B customers and prospects.

2. **This point is a key concept, so keep an open mind. Design your marketing strategy from the bottom-up by seeking input from the field and tailoring your approach to support the unique needs of your local markets and salespersons.** The process imposes a discipline of fact-based capital allocation to your best customers and prospects, and also a simple procedure to measure results. It will also remind you that while tactics come from the field, it is the employees who execute them.

   a. Using a bottom-up marketing strategy, Personalized Marketing Accounts can be established based on the local office or salesperson's potential contribution to your company's revenue and profitability. A good example of this bottom-up approach is Ritz Carlton Hotel allowing its employees immediate discretion to spend up to $2,000 on a customer to uphold the company's reputation for superior customer service; no strings attached.

   b. By contrast, the "top down" creation of marketing strategy and budgets often results in tremendous waste and ineffectuality because every market and every customer is different.

3. **Marketing tactics for your best customers and prospects can be identified and agreed upon with your field offices and sales teams. The field and sales persons are empowered to access their budgets and launch tactics within the agreed upon framework to your best customers and prospects,** *as long as they target the right customers.* Your corporate office, and especially the marketing staff, will serve as a field support organization. While counter-intuitive to most, work to extract the most effort from your sales personel in order to promote a greater balance between empowerment and accountability. The result: greater field & sales team alignment. In sum, it's a dramatically different—*contrarian*—way to market. As Gabriel Shaheen, former CEO of Lincoln National Life Insurance Co., once stated, "The goal of marketing in our business is to make the sales person's job easier."

4. **A data-centric approach to marketing sets the strategy for field offices and sales teams, and is used to allocate the budget to each. The field and sales teams buy-in since they are the ones empowered with their own marketing budget and resources.**

5. **Key Focus Areas and Themes:**

   a. Use data for fact-based decision making in marketing.

   b. Pick your customers before they pick you so that you are not targeting a mass market and ending up with mediocre or "bad" customers. "Acquire your competitors, one customer at a time"—as Michael Dell says.

   c. Don't take a victim approach to marketing. In other words, don't misplace your trust by accepting promises from advertising vendors that may fall through, or by expecting someone else to do all the work. Marketing is too important to leave in the hands of anyone not fully vested in the end result.

   d. Don't engage in mass media or similar "spray & pray" marketing schemes.

To develop your marketing strategy, first understand the patterns within your customer base. Target the customers with whom you are succeeding, and assess whether the patterns are aligned with what you want to achieve. It's called **Pattern Analysis**.

What Is Pattern Analysis?

Simply put, it is a form of data analysis that allows you to segment your market rather than attempt mass marketing. In turn, once you know your segmented group or groups, you can allocate your resources accordingly. Let's say you have 1500 customers. Do you have to market to all of them? Should you? Not if only 10 percent of those customers do 70 percent of your business. Performing a pattern analysis will help you pinpoint that segment of the market that brings the greatest return.

I often find that marketing decision makers gravitate between the two extremes of either (1) over-simplifying why customers do business with their company or (2) getting into the heart of why each individual does business with their company.

Pattern analysis is a happy medium between these extremes, and will help to clarify where you are succeeding.

How does Pattern Analysis work?

It is a relatively simple process if you're familiar with Microsoft Excel, Microsoft Access, or either the Apple version or Goggle Apps version of Excel. If you're not proficient with either, there are affordable outsourcing options to help you (See Resources).

Basically, pattern analysis should focus on the following:

1. What percent of your revenue is generated by the top five percent and 10 percent of your customer base?

2. Using gross margins, what percent of profit is generated by the top five percent and 10 percent of your customer base?

3. How many of these customers transacted with you in the last 30 days?

4. How often do they transact over a 30-day period?

5. What is their average transaction value?

6. What are they buying from you?

7. How much does each one of these customers spend with you annually?

8. What do they look like?

    a. What profession or industry are they in?
    b. How much revenue do their companies generate?
    c. How many employees do they have?
    d. What is their corporate buying process like?
        i. Is it local, multi-unit or headquarters?
    e. How do they use your products and services?

9. Why do you think they transact with you? Goodstein suggests that here you need to employ laddering techniques that move from simple evaluation of the functional benefits derived from your products and services to the emotional and personal benefits your offerings provide the buyer.

    a. What functional, emotional, or self-defining benefits are they trying to elicit?

        i. Flexibility
        ii. Empathy
        iii. Status
        iv. Exclusivity
        v. Competitive Advantage
        vi. Other reasons?

The following page shows an example.

XYZ Company

	Cumulative % of Your Customers	
	Top 5%	Top 6% - 10%
1. Revenue % generated by top customer base?	70%	80%
2. Profit % generated by top customer base?	80%	90%
3. Business transactions with XYZ Company in last 30 days by top base?	100	200
4. How often do they transact business? (30 Day Period)	5	2
5. What is their average transaction value?	$400	$250
6. What do they spend with you annually?	$24,000	$6,000
7. What does their profile look like?		
What industry are they in?	50% Construction, 20% MFG	
What is their average, annual revenue?	$2 million - $5 million	
On average, how many employees do they have?	25 - 50 employees	
What is their buying process? (Local, Headquarters)	Local & Headquarters	
Why do you think they do business with you?	Service, dependable	
What high level feeling are you trying to elicit?	Flexible Exclusivity Dependable	Flexible Dependable

Don't be intimated by the process. You can do this for your business in just a few minutes. If you don't immediately know the answer, go with your best estimate.

What came to mind in the last 60 seconds? Your conclusions will help you on the path forward. Now that you've grouped your customers into patterns, ask yourself whether you like what you see. The answer should be yes.

Often times, we are blinded by our successes and over-magnify our failures. Your data will likely tell you that five percent or ten percent of your customers generate 70 percent or more of your revenue and profits—and if this group of customers represents your "raving fans."

In my business, construction equipment rental, five percent of customers account for 73 percent of revenue and spend about $35,000 each annually. The next five percent of customers account for 10 percent of revenue and spend $8,000 each annually. The top tier clients spend more than four times greater the amount as the next best customers.

Now let's focus on duplicating the success you enjoy with your B-of-B clients. In repeating that success, you will gain confidence in your marketing strategy.

To recap:

• Get to know the profile of your B-of-B customers.

• You can duplicate your success with your B-of-B customers.

• You are allocating the majority of your marketing capital on a B-of-B customer base and any prospects that look just like them.

• Your ability to measure results is now clearer.

Then ask:

• Did you spend your resources and build more loyalty with your top customers?

• Did you grow your customer base with prospects that mirror your B-of-B customers?

Let's apply this same approach to a real life case study that involved one of the most recognizable names in the fast food industry. As you'll see, this major company learned a critical lesson in segmented marketing: that 25 percent of their customers were "super fans," who did 50 percent of the business.

Case Study #4: Burger King Identifies Core Customers and Scores Profit

Burger King ranks second only to McDonald's as a fast-food empire chain. Currently, it has more than 12,000 restaurants in over 70 different countries. But in 2005, sales at Burger King Corp. had plummeted with hundreds of its U.S. restaurants closing, and four of its ten largest franchisees filing for bankruptcy protection. After being run by 11 chief executives and four parent companies throughout two decades, Burger King was in danger of losing its place to Wendy's International, Inc.

Private owners took over and the CEO was replaced with Harvard-trained MBA Greg Brenneman, who moved quickly to improve relationships with franchisees, comprising about 90 percent of the U.S. restaurants. His next step was to identify core customers and give them the products they wanted most.

What drove Burger King, the company soon determined, were "super fans," the 25 percent of the customer base who did 50 percent of the spending, and dined at Burger King 15 or more times per month. Getting just one more visit from the "super fan", was like a ten percent increase in comparable sales. **The goal was to boost the restaurant's annual sales figure from $970,000 to about $1.3 million.**

When the recession took hold in 2009, Burger King slowed its expansion efforts, yet continued to convert and court its customer base of 18-25 year-old male customers. This was the segmented group identified as frequently hungry, loyal, and steady, or "super fans". Unlike the white-collar weight-conscious, these blue-collar workers burned a serious amount of calories on their jobs.

"If you look at the Enormous Omelet Sandwich," said Brenneman, "we didn't beat around the bush with the name. It's an indulgent breakfast item, and it's absolutely geared to our 'super fan'."

Burger King catered to its best customers with items such as the Enormous Omelet Sandwich. They were not trying to be all things to all people.

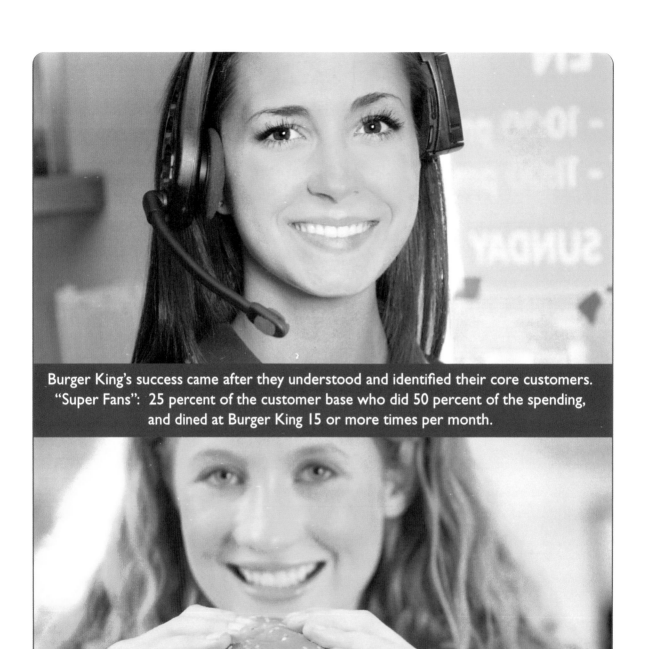

Burger King's success came after they understood and identified their core customers. "Super Fans": 25 percent of the customer base who did 50 percent of the spending, and dined at Burger King 15 or more times per month.

It was not only smart business, but rather a marketing and sales strategy that understood what their particular segmented customers wanted, and then gave it to them. As a result, Burger King was among the few restaurant chains doing well in the pits of the recession.

> *When asked what were the keys to Burger King's turnaround and why the U.S. has room for thousands more Burger Kings, one certified public accountant concluded that it is about identifying the right customer and not wasting time trying to be all things to all people (Wall Street Journal, Dow Jones Reprints, "Man Behind Burger King Turnaround," by J. Adamy 4/02/08).*

The strategy Burger King used was a form of predictive modeling, a way to utilize patterns that identify both risks and opportunities. Credit scoring companies use predictive analysis to determine a customer's rank and the likelihood they will make future payments on time.

Warren Buffett, investor, entrepreneur extraordinaire, and a respected economic voice in any industry, was referring to predictive modeling when he advised Microsoft founder Bill Gates, "to just keep things simple. Boil it down; work on those things that really count; think through the basics. Then it's amazing what you can do." Gates referred to Buffett's advice as "a special form of genius" (*CNBC.com*, by A. Crippen, 06/22/09).

In college, I read the autobiography of Sam Walton, founder of Wal-Mart, who credited his company's success (among many things) to its ability to work faster than the competition. He believed that since customers' interests always changed, and since every market is different, Wal-Mart needed a core competency to test customer interest and identify customer trends. It was essential that they be ready to move quickly when the market shifted.

Wal-Mart has a culture of 'try it, fix it, do it again…rapidly' in which predictive modeling allows them to use data to manage every inch of their business. This data tracking gives them instant information to stay current with customer preferences and changing demands. As a result, their best selling items are always in stock, leading to substantially increased profitability.

From my experience working with other companies, I have found Buffet's advice on developing predictive models helpful. When I have implemented customer relationship management (CRM) systems over the past 10+ years, what I have had in mind was more than just growing a customer base; I wanted to cultivate the right customer base. In other words, I wanted to pick our customers before they picked us.

At Volvo Rents, I focus on the potential profitability of offering customized services in each of our local markets, estimating that 10 percent of the company's customers generate 83 percent of its revenue. I have often told our general managers, "It doesn't matter if a salesperson makes a hundred sales calls. What matters is how many of those calls are connected with the top customers."

> *Just keep things simple.*
> *Boil it down; work on those things that really count; think through the basics.*
> *Then it's amazing what you can do.*
> *—Warren Buffett*

This approach has paid off at Volvo Rents. Our customer base grew by more than 800 percent in six years, from 23,000 in 2003 to 200,000+ in 2010, and the B-of-B high-frequency customers grew by more than 15 times in that same period. We found customers that transacted with us in the highest frequency category spent almost four times more than customers in the next frequency category. *Those* are the customers we want.

Currently, we continue building our loyal base of customers by encouraging our retail stores to provide superior customer service to their best clients. In a nutshell, we have learned to understand and to utilize our strength of focusing on B-of-B customers by analyzing customer data.

In the next chapter, we'll answer some of the more relevant questions on how to spot—and avoid—common traps in marketing techniques. While **Contrarian Marketing** can be a "gold mine" (if the technique is applied properly), You need to be wary of the pitfalls you should definitely avoid.

CONTRARIAN
MARK**E**TING

CHAPTER THREE:
MINING FOR GOLD; WATCHING FOR SINKHOLES

Chapter Three: Mining for Gold; Watching for Sinkholes

> *"Your time is limited, so don't waste it living someone else's life.*
> *Don't be trapped by dogma—which is living with the results*
> *of other people's thinking."*
>
> —Steve Jobs, Apple CEO

If you are like most companies and individuals, you wonder how to market effectively. How do you allocate marketing capital efficiently? How do you decide between different marketing tactics? How do you track results?

The questions in marketing can be endless: which marketing media do you focus on and how much marketing capital do you need? What is the difference in effectiveness between print advertising, online, billboards, events, direct mail, word-of-mouth, TV ads, radio, search engine marketing, even the Yellow Pages?

Furthermore:

1. How much emphasis do you place on your sales team's feedback on marketing?

2. What marketing messages do you communicate to your best customers and prospects?

3. Do you over-focus on a medium in which the sales person of that outlet is most effective or likable?

4. How do you do a "quick fix" on your sales or profitability problems?

5. Does your senior management team give subjective and uncoordinated feedback to the marketing department?

6. Are you over-spending in marketing? How can you tell?

7. Can you track the results of your marketing investments?

8. Are you generally disappointed by the results that you get from your marketing campaigns?

9. How many customers do you really need to be successful?

10.   Do you allow your sales people to attribute their failure to poor marketing?

Later in the book, I'll help you navigate through the confusion by determining if you are successful and the why and how of multiplying your success. But first, it's essential that you understand and avoid four basic traps.

Avoiding the Four Basic Traps:

1. The Ego Trap

A lot of marketing media plays to your ego—putting your name or your company's name 'in lights'. Effective advertising sales staff will aim to flatter you or your company by suggesting that they will make you rich and famous. For example, were you proud when your company advertised on TV or radio for the first time? Or when you launched your first advertising campaign? What about when your logo was featured in the baseball stadium for the first time? It is okay to be proud of your company's success, but hubris is a luxury few companies can afford in these uncertain economic times. Market to your company's strengths and not to your ego.

2. The Competition Trap

Playing the game of 'Your competitor is advertising here….so should you' is common. Tradeshows are infamous for turning marketing spending into an arms race among competitors for who has the largest exhibition space. The biggest winner is not you, nor your competitors to see who can spend the most, but the firm who sold you the space. The most effective marketers aim to be contrarian and to market where their customers/prospects are but their competitors are not.

3. The Messaging Trap

Marketing competes for the precious attention of the customer. By cramming too many messages, or the wrong message, into marketing tactics you vastly lower your chances of capturing your customers' attention and loyalty. Examples of very clear marketing with a singular message vs. those with an obscure message or no message at all include:

–Subway's "Five Dollar Footlong" & healthful eating campaign vs. Quizno's lack of a clear message.

–Coca Cola's refreshing campaign vs. Pepsi's lack of clear message.

–Barack Obama's 'Change' campaign vs. McCain's mixed messages in the last Presidential election.

–Salesforce.com's "No Software" message vs. Microsoft's complex software message.

–BMW's "ultimate driving machine" message to high-end customers (drive our cars and you ARE successful) vs. GM's jack-of-all-trades message, etc.

4. The Customer Trap

This is the largest trap of all….thinking that all customers are the same. If five percent of your customers generate 70 percent of revenue and profits, you should allocate 70 percent of your marketing capital to target those customers and prospects. Moreover, you should design your business processes to treat those customers differently—treat them as B-of-B customers and they will become raving fans.

Many companies also fail by giving the 'moon and stars' to non B-of-B customers and prospects. If a low-value customer asks for special treatment, find a nice way to say 'no'. As an example, my first job out of college was for May Department Stores (May Company), a multi-billion dollar retailer in 1991.

> *Many businesses systematically fail, as soon as they state: "If I make an exception for you, then I have to make exceptions for everyone." Business is not designed for equality—you should constantly make exceptions for your B-of-B customers and prospects. Do not treat all of your customers the same. Treat them all with respect, but treat your best customers the best—always.*

The company had a "no questions" return policy, which many of the low-value customers systematically used it to steal from May Company. We had a warehouse full of men's suits from customers who wore the suits until they were thread-bare, and returned them to the store, claiming the suits were "defective" merchandise. May Department Stores ended up being a retailer characterized by sub-par profitability, went through a series of consolidations, and ultimately was acquired by Federated Department stores (the parent company of Macy's).

Ironically, Nordstrom needs to be careful of going the same route. This past weekend, one of my friends confessed that his wife systemically abuses Nordstrom's return policy by buying expensive dresses for special engagements, and returning them the next day. She even returned a pair of shoes for her son after he had worn them for a year. Of course, she claimed the shoes were defective! I am not proud of this example, but it is relevant to the point.

'Satisfaction Guaranteed' led to sub-par profitability at May Company.

If your customers systematically cheat you, they are thieves, not customers. Fire them. Don't think you can "fire" a customer? Think again. Getting rid of unprofitable customers is exactly what some businesses have learned to do and are now better off for it.

Though there is an ongoing debate about whether companies have the right—or should—"fire" troublesome customers, nearly everyone agrees that if you don't, your more desirable customers will suffer for it.

Next, let's figure out where to begin the process of sifting through your customer base so that you can pick the right customers before they pick you.

> *If your customers systematically cheat you, they are thieves, not customers.*
> *Fire them.*

CONTRARIAN
MARKƎTING

CHAPTER FOUR:
BEGIN WITH THE END IN MIND

Chapter Four: Begin with the End in Mind

> *"In the business world, the rearview mirror is always clearer than the windshield."*
>
> *—Warren Buffett, Investor*

Where is the best place to begin with the end in mind? Start by understanding these basic principles:

1. Successful marketing is 90 percent mathematical and ten percent creative.

Determine how much revenue and profits are generated from the top five percent and ten percent of your customer base and aim to clone your success with this group.

2. Sustaining a marketing campaign on predictable time-frames allows customers to expect information that is consistent and frequent.

The *frequency* of contact with your best customers and prospects is more important than getting "the message" right once. Know *when* to reach out to prospects according to the stages of their decision process.

- Once a week is too often; once a month not enough, according to research firm Marketing Sherpa. How to find the right balance should be based on the buying cycle. For example, with a three-month buying cycle, send content roughly every 15 days, between day 10 and day 75 of the cycle.

- At the beginning and end of each cycle, frequency should increase to every five to 10 days. If that doesn't work well, ask your B-of-B customers how often they would like to be contacted and with what information (To learn more, search for *Marketo's* guide to lead nurturing at www.marketo.com).

Many marketers make the mistake of not sticking to a marketing campaign over the long haul. You should consider all of the friendships you have made in your life, or even the new relationships, in which trust was established through the accumulation of many experiences over time as opposed to "love at first sight."

3. Stick to the basics.

Advertisers have long considered a unique selling proposition (USP) as essential in making their communications actionable with the customer. The idea is that the advertisement must make clear that the product being promoted offers a single, compelling and relevant benefit if it is to change the behavior of the targeted buyer (See Reeves, Rosser (1961), *Reality in Advertising*, New York: Alfred A. Knopf, LCCN 61007118). The same is true of the **Contrarian Marketing** approach. Ideally, focus on one primary message:

a. Coca-Cola: Refreshing

b. Obama: Change

c. Volvo: Safety

d. Nike: Just Do It

e. BMW: Ultimate Driving Machine

Some good current examples of products with a clear USP are (source: Wikipedia):

a. Head & Shoulders: "You get rid of dandruff"

b. Oil of Olay: "You get younger-looking skin"

Some unique propositions that were pioneers when they were introduced:

a. Domino's Pizza: "You get fresh, hot pizza delivered to your door in 30 minutes or less—or it's free."

b. FedEx: "When your package absolutely, positively has to get there overnight."

Advertisers have long considered a unique selling proposition (USP) as essential in making their communications actionable with the customer. Some unique propositions that were pioneers when they were introduced.

Your customers' time and attention span is extremely limited. They are bombarded daily by a non-stop flow of information from their business to their personal lives. Simplify, simplify, simplify your messaging, and you will exponentially multiply the chances that your campaign is remembered.

4. Understand the Concept of Cost per Impression to evaluate marketing investments.

In many cases, marketers or business people gravitate to the wrong marketing media because their decision-making is over-influenced by what they are familiar with in their personal lives.

For example, TV has historically been one of the most powerful influencers of customer behavior because it's engaging and has the ability to cover vast geographic areas. However, if your company is only targeting a few thousand customers within a market, why pay for impressions with the hundreds or thousands or millions who don't have a need to ever purchase your company's products or services?

Marketing: Why pay for impressions with hundreds or thousands or maybe millions who don't have a need to ever purchase your company's products or services?

BILLBOARD

MAIL

SPAM

TV

INTERNET

TELEMARKETING

In many cases, marketers or business people gravitate to the wrong marketing media because their decision-making is over-influenced by what they are familiar with in their personal lives.

A primary example of this type of error was made by MCI (when it was still a well-respected carrier) in approaching the B2B marketplace. In the early 1990s, MCI decided to expand its target market beyond customer households and into the business arena. Executives of the company determined that recruiting one major business to the MCI family would equal the revenues of thousands of households. They developed an advertisement that focused on surprising business customers about how many companies already are part of the MCI family. The ad showed an MCI executive on Wall St. touting the many firms that use MCI by having their logos join MCI on the Street. The ad scored very well with business prospects. The decision, however, to run the ad during Monday Night Football meant that millions of

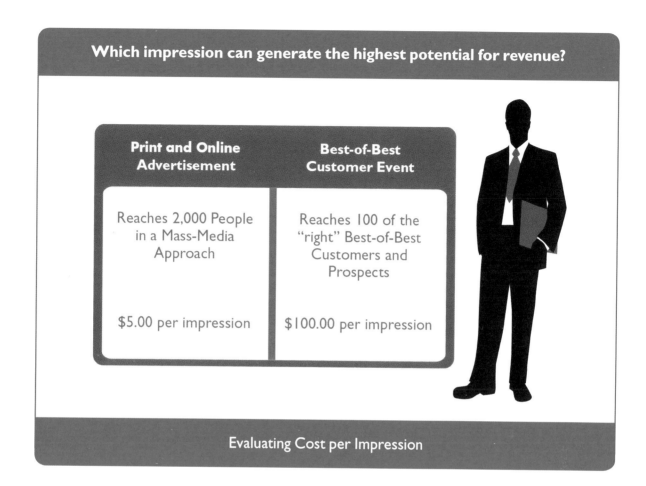

Which impression can generate the highest potential for revenue?

Print and Online Advertisement	Best-of-Best Customer Event
Reaches 2,000 People in a Mass-Media Approach	Reaches 100 of the "right" Best-of-Best Customers and Prospects
$5.00 per impression	$100.00 per impression

Evaluating Cost per Impression

non-targeted customers were exposed to the ad. What happened Tuesday morning was that a record number of household customers switched from MCI to AT&T, as they believed that MCI was no longer going to serve them as part of their B-of-B set.

How do you calculate "cost per impression"? (This is defined as the cost to get your message to each person). Here are a couple of examples:

a. If a print and online advertisement costs $10,000 and reaches 2,000 people: the cost per impression is $5 ($10,000 divided by 2,000).

b. If a "Best of Best" customer event costs $10,000 and entertains 100 people: the cost per impression is $100 ($10,000 divided by $100).

5. Understand the Concept of 'Cost per Qualified Lead':

There is an important distinction between a <u>qualified prospect</u> and an <u>unqualified prospect</u>. Your focus, of course, should be on the qualified. A qualified prospect reasonably has the potential to purchase your product or service. As an example of seeking qualified prospects, Gulfstream Aviation, a manufacturer of private jets, once advertised frequently in the *Wall Street Journal* since the publication had a high concentration of readers that were CEOs and high net worth individuals. By contrast, Gulfstream is unlikely to ever advertise on TV as they would be paying to reach a vast amount of people who could never afford to purchase their premium product.

An unqualified prospect costs you in two ways:

    a. The cost to market to an unqualified prospect.

    b. The organizational resource (time spent by your staff) cost to learn that the prospect is not qualified.

Which is more cost effective?

    a. Print advertisement in your local newspaper:
    Cost = $10,000
    Reaches 2,000 prospects.
    Reaches 50 qualified prospects in a very low-impact way.

    Cost per qualified prospect = $200 ($10,000 divided by 50)

    b. First-class event for B-of-B customers
    Cost = $10,000
    Reaches 100 highly qualified prospects in a very high-impact, high-touch way

    Cost per qualified prospect = $100 ($10,000 divided by 100)

In this scenario print advertising is twice as expensive as event marketing.

Based on your judgment, if your B-of-B prospects have the potential to spend $20,000 per year with your company, which marketing tactic (a one-time newspaper ad or a one-time first-class event) is more likely to help you in earning a relationship with that prospect? I hope you guessed right: the first-class event.

6. **Be contrarian, spend your marketing funds where customers are, where your company is strong, and where your competition is weak.** For example, if your competition mass-markets, grab their best customers with a highly focused marketing campaign to that group. If your company has exceptionally strong service, make a bold guarantee to your B-of-B customers and prospects that your company guarantees a specific service-level or the service is free. Be simple, clear, and bold.

Use different marketing tactics than what your competition employs. For instance, if your competition gives away logo merchandise as a customer incentive (e.g., shirts, pens, hats, etc.), use a gift service to send thoughtful gift baskets with personalized notes.

In companies that I have worked with in the past, I have commissioned company-specific, branded "Tiffany-style" quality boxes for $10 each. While some may regard a $10 box as wasteful, the company creates tremendous break-through and excitement with customers who receive a gift that is elegantly packaged. A box is filled and sent with items tailored to the customer's specific tastes, whether it is cookies, a bottle of wine, or gourmet peanuts. A personalized note is also included. As a result, the company has received countless unsolicited phone calls from customers thanking them for their thoughtfulness.

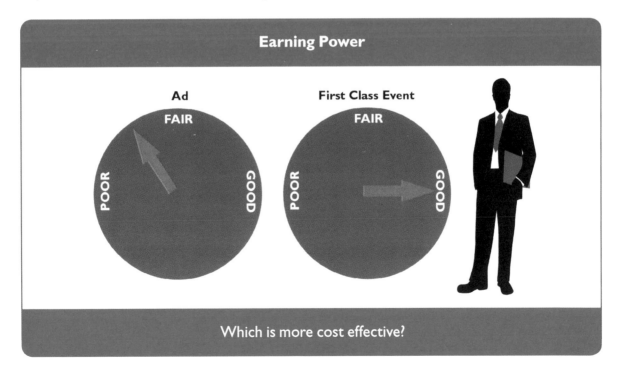

59

Here's a testimonial from an employee who received outstanding returns by sending out gifts to B-of-B customers:

"I sent out customer gifts recently," says Fernando A., and included a prospect that we've been trying to turn into a customer for the past year. When he received his gifts he called to thank us. After that, he placed an order for $3,000."

Where else can you get that type of return on your investment?

> *"When he received his gifts, he called to thank us.*
> *After that, he placed an order for $3,000."*

7. Decide whether your company wants to be all things to all people

Both Wal-Mart and Nordstrom have viable and profitable business models—however each has vastly different customer propositions: "low prices" to the masses (Wal-Mart) and "great service" to the few who can afford their prices (Nordstrom).

8. **Align your marketing initiatives directly with your sales initiatives by sharing a specific list of target customers and prospects with your sales team, and developing the value proposition together.**

   In business-to-business marketing, the marketing is designed to support the sales force. The marketing department and sales department should never be adversarial. By working from a common list, and developing the USP together, the marketing and sales teams can consolidate their efforts as a force multiplier for superior results.

9. **Align your marketing messaging with the customer experience that your operation delivers.**

   It is essential that the customers who buy your product or service have the "experience" that your company's marketing campaigns promise.

   Marketing is very, very simple:
   —A company makes a promise.
   —A customer has an expectation to receive what is promised.

10. **Focus only on a few B-of-B customers and prospects so you can pick your customers and prospects before they pick you.**

    Targeting the few not only enables you to re-write the rule-book on cost per impression and cost per lead, but also enables you to bring quality and confidence to your entire team—from the CEO suite, to field offices and your sales staff.

> *Marketing is very, very simple:*
>   *—A company makes a promise.*
>   *—A customer has an expectation to receive what is promised.*

In most markets, broadcast or print media deliver the message with greater than 95 percent waste. In other words, more than 95 percent of the recipients of the message are *not* potential customers. These media inefficiencies make it impossible to get a good deal and expect a reasonable return on investment.

For this reason, I discourage local stores and salespersons from such an inefficient methodology. Far more efficient are the concerted efforts to build bottom-up marketing campaigns personalized to each local market and salesperson, and most importantly, to each customer.

In the next chapter, I'll present the method and merits of determining just how many customers you really need.

CONTRARIAN
MARK**E**TING

CHAPTER FIVE:
A STARTING POINT–QUANTIFYING
"BEST-OF-BEST" PROSPECTS

Chapter Five: A Starting Point—Quantifying 'Best-of-Best' Prospects

> *"I like to go for cinches. I like to shoot fish in a barrel.*
> *But I like to do it after the water has run out."*
>
> —*Warren Buffett, investor*

The starting point of every marketing campaign should quantify the number and type of prospective customers you want to acquire. In addition, the target prospect list should spell out the names of which prospects you want to acquire as your customers.

For those of you that are math-averse, stay with me. The process is neither as complex nor intimidating as it sounds. I'll demonstrate how you can accomplish this task through a few simple steps, and in less time than what you spend at work going to lunch.

A Basic Customer and Prospect Intelligence System

Let's begin with an example from the XYZ Company.

1. XYZ has 150,000 customers in its 50 store network. Per store, only 500 of these customers are "active"—having transacted in the last 180 days.

2. Of the above group of 500 customers per store, the top five percent of customers generate 75 percent of revenue and profits. These B-of-B customers each spend $30,000 per year. (Below, I will show you a simple technique to create a simple table of customer data so you can view your customer base in easy-to-understand patterns.)

3. Multiplying five percent x 500 = 25 B-of-B customers per store.

XYZ has 150,000 customers in its 50 store network. Per store, only 500 of these customers are "active"—having transacted in the last 180 days.

This is a way to use an easy technique that goes from complex to simple in a few minutes. In this case, I reduced 150,000 customers for the entire company to identifying 25 B-of-B customers per store—*those that really count.*

The merits and implications of acquiring 25 additional B-of-B customers are as follows:

- The clarity and efficiencies derived from focusing on marketing to a few prospects, as opposed to the entire market.

- The top five percent of customers (25 customers) generate 75 percent of revenue (25 customers X $30,000 = $750,000 in revenue annually).

- The remaining 95 percent of customers generate 25 percent of revenue (475 customers times $600 annual spend each = $285,000 in revenue)

- Which group would you rather focus on, the top five percent or the remaining 95 percent?

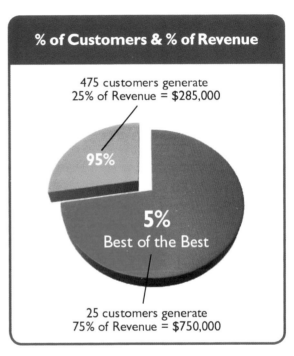

% of Customers & % of Revenue

475 customers generate
25% of Revenue = $285,000

95%

5%
Best of the Best

25 customers generate
75% of Revenue = $750,000

If you want to have the largest impact on your business, you simply need to target and attract 25 prospects that look and behave just like your B-of-B customers. Doing so will create $750,000 in revenue (25 new customers times $30,000 each = $750,000). This equates to a 75 percent increase in revenue.

If just ten of those customers were extracted from the competition, your competitor would experience a substantial decrease in revenue and operating profit. Which could possibly have a catastrophic outcome on their business.

| | Avg. annual spend/customer | |
	Best of the Best	95% Group
1 More Customer	$30,000	$600
2 More Customers	$60,000	$1,200
3 More Customers	$90,000	$1,800

If you do not know how much revenue and profitability that the top five percent of your customers generate, I will show you a simple technique that has been around for years, and will enable you to quickly group your customer data into patterns that you can easily recognize.

Let's spend a few minutes going through the following exercise:

Segmenting Your Customer Data

Let's start with a simple graphic that explains the primary purpose in segmentation, then move on to an exercise. Notice that Customer 1 and Customer 6 are high revenue generators for this business.

Now if we take our customer data and break it down, we find these two customers drive a lot of revenue for this business.

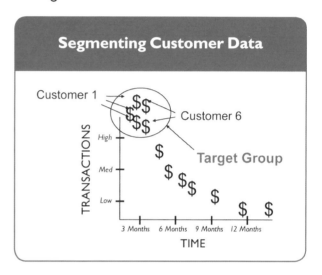

	Transactions	Lifetime Transactions	Frequency (if transaction in past 30 Days)	Recency (Days)	Value Range
Customer 1	3	45	3	3 in 0-30	$12,000-$17,000
Customer 6	2	55	2	2 in 0-30	$9,000-$11,999

Next we will apply segmentation principles in an exercise.

1. Start with an electronic list of your customers (for example, export your customer list to Microsoft Excel) with their life-to-date transaction history (date, item, amount, etc.). You may have thousands of customers accounting for tens of thousands of transactions with your business. If the above is too intimidating, use the data from just one of your locations or one of your sales persons. A random sample of your company's data is highly likely to be a representative sample for your entire company.

2. Use Microsoft Excel to sort the data by customer (primary) and transaction amount (secondary).

3. Subtotal the data by customer. For each customer, this determines the number of transactions, $ per transaction and total revenue.

4. To group your data into patterns, you will need to establish a simple table of Recency, Frequency and Monetary values (RFM).

What is RFM?

RFM is used to formulate action-based target segments by examining the purchase behavior of your current customer set. It explores when, how often, and in what dollar quantities customers make their purchases.

Utilize the sort function by accessing the 'Data' menu in Microsoft's Excel.

Think of it like the workhorse of value-based segmentation.

> **R**= the length of time since a customer's last purchase
>
> **F**= the number of times a purchase was made
>
> **M**=the amount of money spent within a certain period

Regarding the recommended segmentations for Recency, Frequency and Monetary below, tailor these as they apply to your business.

Note: RFM is explained in detail in Chapter Seven.

5. **Recency** can also be defined as the time frame between orders.

Recency values are determined by the last time your customer transacted. I recommend the following breaks by number of days:
i. 0-30
ii. 31-60
iii. 61-90
iv. 91-180
v. and 181-365

6. **Frequency** is how many orders have been placed over time.

Frequency values are determined by the number of times a customer transacts over his lifetime with your business. I recommend:
i. 24+
ii. 12-23
iii. 6-11
iv. 5, 4, 3, 2, and 1.

7. **Monetary** is the value of the sum of the orders over time.

Monetary values are determined by summing all of a customer's transactions with your business over a lifetime. I recommend:

i. $25,000+
ii. $20,000-$24,999
iii. $15,000-$19,999
iv. $10,000-$14,999
v. $5,000-$9,999

vi. $4,000-$4,999
vii. $3,000-$3,999
viii. $2,000-$2,999
ix. $1,000-$1999
x. $0-$1,000

In our workshop and facilitated training, I recommend detailed breakdowns to the level suggested above. For the examples in our book, we have simplified these breakdowns with a smaller set of customers, transactions, and revenue.

8. Add the **Recency, Frequency** and **Monetary** (RFM) values to the subtotals noted in Step 3. An example is found on the next page.

9. Subtotal the data noted in Step 3. You will now be able to calculate the percent of customers and percent of revenue for your customers based on RFM values.

An example RFM table below shows that on a "frequency basis", nine percent of the customers generate 85 percent of the company's revenue.

'Table' view of RFM data. This is an expert view of customer data. A graphical view of the data on the page after next will be easier for most to act on.

Recency (Days)	Customers	Trans	$/Tran	Revenue	%/Cust	%/Rev	$/Cust
0-30	50	5200	$165	$704,000	5%	63%	$14,080
31-60	35	2700	$70	$192,000	4%	17%	$5,490
61-90	170	450	$57	$80,000	17%	7%	$470
91-120	230	400	$45	$48,000	23%	4%	$210
121-365+	515	1250	$40	$90,000	52%	8%	$175
Total	1000	10,000		$1,114,000	100%		

Frequency (Trans)	Customers	Trans	$/Tran	Revenue	%/Cust	%/Rev	$/Cust
+24	51	5100	$155	$750,000	5%	67%	$14,700
12-23	38	2600	$70	$200,000	4%	18%	$5,260
6-11	165	400	$50	$70,000	17%	6%	$425
5	225	300	$35	$40,000	23%	4%	$175
Under 5 Transactions	521	1600	$20	$54,000	52%	5%	$105
Total	1000	10,000		$1,114,000	100%		

Monetary ($)	Customers	Trans	$/Tran	Revenue	%/Cust	%/Rev	$/Cust
20,000+	49	4600	$140	$725,000	5%	65%	$14,800
15,000-19,999	40	2700	$75	$220,000	4%	4%	$5,500
10,000-14,999	150	900	$70	$60,000	15%	15%	$400
5,000-9,999	175	650	$60	$39,000	18%	18%	$225
Under $5,000	695	1150	$55	$70,000	59%	59%	$120
Total	1000	10,000		$1,114,000	100%		

Here are a few more questions as to how RFM segmentation applies to your business:

1. Recency:

a. How many customers have transacted with you in the last 30 days?

b. Based on a Recency score of 0-30, what percentage of your total customer base do they represent and what percentage of your total revenue base do they represent?

2. Frequency:

a. How many customers do you have that have 24+ transactions in the past year?

b. Based on a Frequency score of 24+, what percentage of your total customer base do they represent and what percent of your total revenue do they represent?

c. Looking at 24+ customers, how much do they spend with you annually on average?

Now that you've had a chance to analyze your businesses' data, do you have a better idea about which customers are generating the majority of your revenue and profit? Note that for specific industries augmentations might be made to improve the segmentation model suggested by RFM. For instance, the consulting firm Harte-Hanks recommends that all segmentation methods begin with a basic RFM analysis. Yet there may be other variables unique to industries that are worth tracking. In retailing, for example, Harte-Hanks suggests that retailers track the longevity of customer transactions, dollars spent in children's sections of the store, and the number of different methods of payment as additional segmentation variables to the basic RFM.

How Do You Tie Your Company's Financial Plan to Your Customer Goals?

On the next page, I graphed the distribution of the percent of customers and percent of revenue based on Recency, Frequency, and Monetary (RFM) values.

By presenting the data graphically, you immediately notice the disproportionate distribution between the percent of customers and the percent of revenue on the left-hand side of the graph.

In this example, the customers who transact 24+ times per year account for five percent of the customers, generate 67 percent of the revenue and spend $14,700 each per year.

The next customer group which transacts 12-23 times per year accounts for four percent of the customers, generate 18 percent of the revenue, and spends $5,260 each (almost three times less than the B-of-B customers). Interestingly, 52 percent of the customers generate only five percent of total revenue.

Where would you rather spend your company's precious time and resources? With the nine percent of customers who drive 85 percent of revenue? Or with the 52 percent of customers who account for five percent of revenue?

As your company, your field offices, or your sales persons plan their revenue and profitability targets for next quarter or next year, the frequency distribution graph of your existing customer base immediately provides you with a solid starting point to determine the requirements for growth with your existing customer base and new customers.

In the next steps, your marketing and sales teams could make a list of the target names of prospective customers that will drive your growth according to your financial plan.

For example, if your business wanted to grow its revenue base from $1.1 million per year to $1.6 million per year (+$500,000) simply focusing on adding 25 B-of-B customers (25 customers x $14,700 each = approximately $370,000) would create 74 percent of the revenue required to achieve the company's goal.

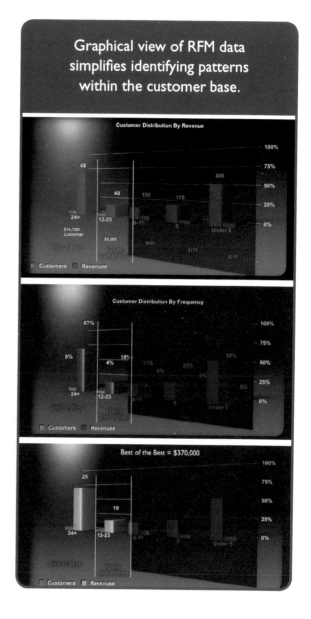

Graphical view of RFM data simplifies identifying patterns within the customer base.

Though it may look complicated, the process is simple. Any company can easily turn its financial targets into a *quantifiable* customer acquisition target.

More specifically, the analysis of your company's data should reveal that your B-of-B customers represent a small percentage of your customer base and a large percentage of your revenue and profits. By focusing your company's efforts on *what has made you succeed*, you greatly enhance your likelihood of success.

To summarize, can you think of the top prospective customers within your company that will generate 70 percent+ of your success if you wanted to grow your business substantially?

> *Can you think of the top prospective customers within your company that will generate 70 percent + of your success?*

Would you have greater confidence in your marketing expenditures if you knew that more than 70 percent of your marketing and sales capital was focused on your B-of-B customers and prospects?

Don't you agree that marketing suddenly becomes much less confusing when you realize that you are not targeting the mass universe of customers, but rather a small percentage that will determine your success?

In the next chapter, we'll talk about evidence-based decisions and I'll explain two things:

1. How you can move from opaque, non-specific marketing goals to an extremely specific list of targets and prospects.

2. How to leverage data to determine the attributes of your best customers and future best customers.

Would you have greater confidence in your marketing expenditures if you knew that more than 70 percent of your marketing and sales capital was focused on your B-of-B customers and prospects?

CONTRARIAN
MARK∃TING

CHAPTER SIX:
FACT BASED DECISION MAKING

Chapter Six: Fact-Based Decision-Making

> *"In God we trust; all others bring data."*
>
> —W. Edwards Deming, Quality Control Expert

With just a few steps you can accurately learn a profile of your customers, your B-of-B customers, and create a prospect list that enables you to target-market with laser-like precision.

Data is critical to fact-based decision making in marketing. Once you've determined how many B-of-B customers you need for a material impact on your business, the next most important step is to establish a profile of the type of customer you are seeking.

Enriching Your Customer Data

To begin, data reporting agencies such as Experian, InfoUSA and Dun & Bradstreet capture immense amounts of information on every customer and business. To some, these agencies may hint at George Orwell's "Big Brother" concept from *Nineteen Eighty-Four*, his classic work on a fictional totalitarian society, but they do provide consolidated information including:

- Credit reports
- Government records
- Magazine subscriptions
- Credit card purchases
- Property values
- Company revenues
- Number of employees
- And… much, much, more.

Data reporting agencies such as Experian, InfoUSA and Dun and Bradstreet capture immense amounts of information on every customer and business.

This data is synthesized and attached to consumer/business records to provide a vast array of intelligence information to marketers. Their mechanisms give you valuable insights on your customers: the type of business, standard industry codes (SIC), revenue, number of employees, ownership info, title, what assets they own, and more. While your company no doubt has a lot of internal customer data for insights, choosing target markets (as in your best customers) usually requires obtaining data from outside sources.

In just a few steps using the data from some of these sources, you can gain valuable insight on your B-of-B customers that will assist you in recognizing patterns and selecting possible variables that may augment the RFM approach.

To begin the process, try following three steps. (For additional help see the Resources page at the end of this book.)

Three-Step Process for Appending Third-Party Data to Your Customer Database

1. Export your customer data with the Recency, Frequency and Monetary (RFM) scores from Chapter Five.

'Table' view of RFM data. This is an expert view of customer data. A graphical view of the data on the next page will be easier for most to act on.

Company	Contact	Revenue 2009	Revenue 2010	Revenue Last 12 Months	Lifetime Revenue	Lifetime Transactions	Recency	Frequency	Monetary Value
Company A	John A.	$8,355	$2,320	$9,790	$10,675	22	03) 31 - 60	02) 12 - 23	04) 10,000 - 14,999
Company B	John B.	$1,665	$3,765	$5,430	$5,430	14	02) 0 - 30	02) 12 - 23	06) 5,000 - 7,499
Company C	John C.	$2,180	$2,108	$4,288	$4,288	19	03) 31 - 60	02) 12 - 23	07) 4,000 - 4,999
Company D	John D.	$38,230	$7,155	$43,135	$45,385	27	03) 31 - 60	01) 24+	01) 25,000+
Company E	John E.	$17,770	$23,815	$37,860	$41,585	34	03) 31 - 60	01) 24+	01) 25,000+
Company F	John F.	$1,725	$18,445	$20,170	$20,170	17	02) 0 - 30	02) 12 - 23	02) 20,000 - 24,999
Company G	John G.	$5,420	$14,575	$19,995	$19,995	40	02) 0 - 30	01) 24+	03) 15,000 - 19,999
Company H	John H.	$1,765	$26,874	$28,639	$28,639	24	03) 31 - 60	01) 24+	01) 25,000+

2. Send your customer data to a market research firm. (You can submit a request or inquiry through our website at www.contrarianmarketingstrategy.com for recommendations.) Market research firms will run your database of customers against their database of businesses and customers and summarize their findings.

   a. For the cost of $0.25–$0.50 per record, their database will match business and/or customer records to your customer database. Based on your direction, they will add Standard Industry Code (SIC) information, company size revenue, location, number of employees, and other data to your customer database. Additional customer attributes can be added, but I recommend the above in order to get you started.

3. Within a few days they will return your customer database to you, with valuable information attached to every customer record.

From this analysis, you will learn what percent of your business is derived from: types of businesses by SIC, number of employees, revenue and location information.

Now check for the *most important patterns* within your customer base. Here's an example of XYZ Business and conclusions from the data:

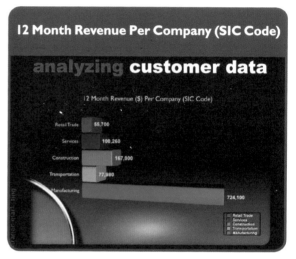

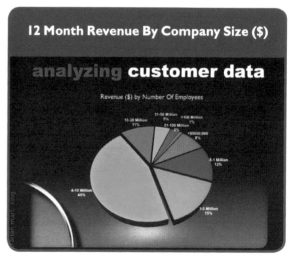

Conclusions:

- Manufacturing companies account for two-thirds (2/3) of revenue. The next largest category is Construction.

- Manufacturing companies lead in revenue per company. Construction follows, along with Service and Transportation.

- Companies with 20-50 employees are the leading revenue producers, with 45 percent of revenue. Other small companies are also major revenue generators, with 91 percent of revenue originating from locations with 100 employees or less.

- Customer Annual Sales Volume data shows the prominence of smaller customers. $4-$10 million annual sales customers comprise the largest segment, closely followed by those from $500,000-$3 million.

Using XYZ Business as an example, this same analysis yields the following insights:

- Manufacturing customers represent 64 percent of revenue.

- Non-Manufacturing businesses represent 36 percent of revenue.

- Companies with 10-50 employees represent 60 percent of revenue.

- Entrepreneur-owned businesses are the best customers.

- B-of-B customers spend on average $14,700 per year and $155 per transaction.

This data enables XYZ to establish a profile of its B-of-B customers. **To create a prospect list that mirrors your B-of-B customers, return to the data reporting agencies and ask them to provide a prospect list based on the main conclusions noted above.**

For a better understanding of data-based results, baseball enthusiasts might relate to Michael Lewis' book *Moneyball: The Art of Winning an Unfair Game* (2003) in which Lewis explains how one of the poorest teams in baseball, the Oakland Athletics, achieved an amazing record over much better funded teams.

The team's general manager, Billy Beane, believed that wins could be had by more affordable standards. He and his staff used massive amounts of statistical data to prove it. They studied outstanding play-by-plays, adding and subtracting players throughout the summer of 2002. With

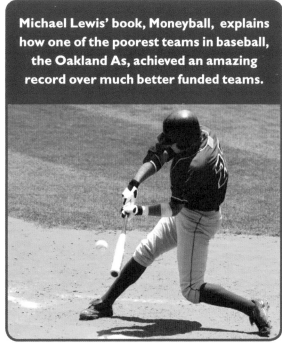

Michael Lewis' book, Moneyball, explains how one of the poorest teams in baseball, the Oakland As, achieved an amazing record over much better funded teams.

Avid golfers constitute 23% of all players and generate 63% of spending on fees and equipment.

his uncanny ability to find the "right" players that he coveted, and know who was likely to be traded, Beane got the best players at the cheapest cost, creating a highly motivated team that despite its financial status, ended up with a spectacular winning season.

If golf is your game, (600,000 people in the U.S. make their living from it) here's what Joe Steranka, CEO of the Professional Golfers' Association of America, has to say about segmenting customers to retain B-of-B.

"Any practical business needs more time with its current customers than in wooing potential customers. It's a more efficient way of doing business," said Steranka.

Avid golfers constitute **23 percent of all players and generate 63 percent of spending** on fees and equipment, according to the National Golf Foundation.

Marketing experts say the golfing industry should be gathering statistics and compiling research on the "best practices" that its members can use at the facility level to *retain existing customers*.

American Express (AmEx) is one of the world's largest travel agencies, though it is better known for its bread and butter charge cards. (Warren Buffett owns about 13 percent of AmEx through Berkshire Hathaway). Ranked seventh out of 31 among its peers as the most admired Fortune 1000 companies in 2008, AmEx recently announced it can now customize business insights through its massive database of customer transaction data, insights designed to help steer marketing decisions and determine overall strategy.

The powerful weapon AmEx is unleashing: transaction information on its 90 million member cardholders to its partner merchants. This detailed data will help marketers determine where to advertise, where to put new stores, and what model would best draw a positive response to services or offers. A customer likes to swim so will they join a health club with a pool? Or will they buy swimwear? Joining a swim club is predictive, and buying swim gear is even more so. It is transactional, predictive data at its best.

> *AmEx's detailed data will help marketers determine where to advertise, where to put new stores, and what model would best draw a positive response to services or offers.*

"Our data is unique as no one else has this level of detail," said Bill Glenn, president of Global Merchant Services at AmEx. "Other companies are doing lifestyle segmentation and modeling, but we're doing modeling off of transaction-level data" (*Advertising Age*, "AmEx Opens up Data Treasure Trove," 2009).

Banking executives have realized for years that a small proportion of customers represent the majority of net revenues and have the advantage of a rich customer database to identify the highest value customer.

One bank utilized its in-house tools to differentiate its customers and develop more targeted sales strategies: In 2006, the Royal Bank of Canada (RBC in Toronto) with assets of $469 billion Canadian, combed through its customer records supported by sales trend data.

American Express is unleashing transaction information on its 90 million member cardholders to its partner merchants.

The records showed there was a whole new segment of higher level customers who previously were under the radar: medical school students and interns. Within a year of targeting these potential high earners, RBC saw this segment's revenue climb to nearly four times that of the "average" customer.

Another bank, Citizens, in Providence, Rhode Island, selected law firms as its most profitable new segment due to high checking account balances, trust accounts, and escrow accounts they maintained. Their forward-thinking led them to target the legal market and establish customized packages of products and services.

> **B-of-B customers value quality service, problem solving, and personal attention more than they do low prices.**

But too often companies make the mistake of leveraging price to gain new customers when they would be better off targeting segments of their existing customer base. It has been demonstrated time and again that many, if not most B-of-B customers value quality service, problem solving, and personal attention more than they do low prices.

In summary, fact-based decision making is not hard when you group customer patterns and take a close look at the data. Basically, you're establishing a profile of the type customer you want to identify and retain. Check for important patterns within the customer base and change your strategy if necessary.

Not pursuing the data is a like embarking on a complex journey without a clear idea of where you are headed, or why—a highly risky endeavor.

Next, let's look at how to go about creating and achieving quantifiable goals that you can actually measure.

CONTRARIAN
MARK∃TING

CREATING QUANTIFIABLE MARKETING GOALS

Chapter Seven: Creating Quantifiable Marketing Goals

> *"We just focus on a few outstanding companies.*
> *We're focus investors."*
>
> —*Warren Buffett, investor*

Marketing is achieved inch by inch, and sometimes seems like a great deal of effort. But now that you've learned a few techniques to determine how many of the B-of-B customers you have, the rest is relatively easy.

First:

1. Identify how important your customers are in creating a substantial portion of your revenue. What percentage did they contribute to your profit margin?

2. Ask: "What do these customers look like?" (What type industry, company size, credit rating, etc. do they have?) Analyze their transactions as well to determine behavioral commonalities.

3. Finally, decide how you can use your customer profile for a list of prospects that will, in the end, be your B-of-B clients.

Before we go much further, it's also important that you take a few minutes to set goals for your B-of-B customers and prospects in your Recency, Frequency, and Monetary (RFM) table as defined in Chapter Five.

Ronald Goodstein, Ph.D, Georgetown University, calls RFM "a powerful predictor of behavior." It uses easily available data, he says, requires no extensive statistical knowledge, is cheap, fast, and flexible, works in business-to-business as well as business-to-consumer, and applies directly to current customers rather than prospects.

How RFM Works:
Used in direct marketing by some of the largest and most successful companies in the world, RFM is based on both reasoning and empirical-based customer behavior. For example, if someone bought from you recently, they are more inclined to respond to a new offer than a customer that bought long ago. Any company with a

customer database can track this type of purchase history, including most recent purchase date. The data is sorted by date, and the top 20 percent is identified with a code, followed by the next 20 percent, etc.

At the end, every customer is coded. This is *recency*. You can also code your customers' *frequency* by tracking their number of transactions in any given time frame (monthly, quarterly, yearly). The *monetary* code is tracked by dollar sales over the same period of time.

All too often companies measure their performance in the aggregate: "We had a good year and delivered $400,000 in profits," or "We made a profit of $2.50 per customer." This is useful information but it does not account for the fact that <u>not all customers are created equal</u>, and some are even unprofitable. Instead of measuring the "average" customer, your business can learn a lot more by determining exactly what each customer brings to the bottom line (*University of Virginia Darden School Foundation*, Charlottesville, VA, 2005).

In short, RFM remains a valuable tool when you want quick success, as it is designed to produce rapid, profitable results (*Marketing Tools*," Boosting Response with RFM," by A. Hughes, May 1996, Vol. 3, Issue 3).

For your purposes, how many B-of-B customers do you have now, and how many new "best" customers do you want over the next twelve (12) months? I would recommend that you aim to grow your "best" customer-base by 25 percent to 50 percent. As an example, I have referenced the data for a highly profitable (fictitious) business.

'Acme' generates over $50 Million annually and has 50 percent EBITDA margins. A common investor term related to the cash flow of a business, EBITDA margin refers to earnings before interest, taxes, depreciation, and amortization as a percent of total revenue. It is a good benchmark of ROI.

Currently, the business example to the right has 470 B-of-B customers. They account for 12 percent of the customer base and generate 87 percent of total revenue.

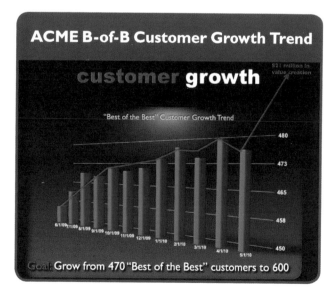

Your goal: grow from 470 B-of-B customers to 600.

Annualized Spending: how much do the B-of-B customers currently spend with you and how much do you want your "cloned best" to spend with you going forward? (Here's a tip: you want your "best" prospects to achieve the same level of spending as your B-of-B customers.)

Acme's B-of-B customers currently spend $96,000 each, annually. There is significant economic value to be created by growing the annual spend by $8,000 each from $96,000 to $104,000.

How often do B-of-B customers transact with you yearly, and how often do you want similar prospects to transact with you going forward? (Tip: you want these prospects to achieve at least the same level of transactions as your B-of-B customers.)

Value Created by Growing Best of Best Customers

	Number of Customers	Transactions Per Year	$/ Transaction	$/ Customer	Revenue
Current Best of the Best Customers	470	120	$800	$96,000	$45,120,000
Increase in Spend by Current B-of-B Customers	470	130	$800	$104,000	$ 3,760,000
Value Created by New B-of-B Customers	130	130	$800	$104,000	$13,520,000
Total Value Creation	600				$17,280,000

As an example, Acme B-of-B customers transact 120 times per year on average. This business aims to grow transactions to 130 times per year at $800 each.

When Acme achieves the goals outlined above, it will have created approximately $17 million in value creation: $3.8 Million from existing customers and $13.5 million from converting the target list of prospects to new "best" customers.

By focusing on these few customers, and the prospects that look just like them (clones), Acme exerted highly focused efforts to have a material impact on its business. Any Chief Financial Officer (CFO) and Chief Executive Officer (CEO) would love the results.

You now have quantifiable goals that you can visualize with a tremendous amount of detail.

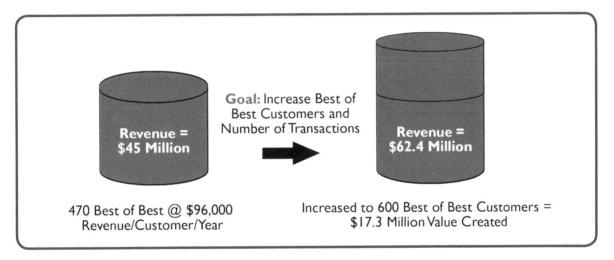

Goal: Increase Best of Best Customers and Number of Transactions

Revenue = $45 Million

Revenue = $62.4 Million

470 Best of Best @ $96,000 Revenue/Customer/Year

Increased to 600 Best of Best Customers = $17.3 Million Value Created

Your Chief Financial Officer or accounting team should be "singing your praises" since you are speaking their language: the language of numbers. By setting goals for your B-of-B customers and prospects, you can track your results and progress with tremendous accuracy.

In the December 2007 issue of *Deliver Magazine* (a publication for Marketing Professionals), I was interviewed for a feature story on how marketers "are learning to speak a language that only a Chief Financial Officer could love."

Deliver Magazine: **The highly acclaimed publication from the U.S. Postal Service for Marketing Professionals.**

In their story, they first captured the past by pointing out that marketers once had only a few basic questions to ask, from "What are my customers like?" to "How can I help them?" But today, the questions are radically different.

Among the things marketers need to know now are how effective their marketing efforts are, and how that effectiveness can be measured; what's the budget for advertising, e-marketing, direct mail, and other needed elements; where can you trim costs to improve the bottom line without compromising your effectiveness?

In addition, companies' chief financial officers are now driven by increased scrutiny on bookkeeping and a desire for market growth. And while CFOs are an audience many marketers aren't used to addressing, a strong relationship between marketing and the CFO should be nurtured.

Yet requests for this accountability often go unanswered. According to a November 2005 study by the Chief Marketing Officer Council, just 49 percent of companies with revenues over $500 million reported using formal marketing performance scorecards. Smaller companies report using performance scorecards only 20 percent of the time, although 58 percent claim to have a scorecard under development. This dearth of knowledge led an international panel of marketing academics and practitioners to rank "returns on marketing investment" as one of the priority research areas for the field (Marketing Science Institute Research Priorities 2008-2010).

Quantifiable marketing goals enable the entire enterprise to work together, building trust and empowerment throughout the company. What it comes down to is two-way communication.

The marketing team at Volvo Rents, a Volvo Group subsidiary launched in 2001, knows this well. The team habitually lavishes gifts—from $50 cookie tins to auto race tickets—on their preferred customers.

> *Quantifiable marketing goals enable the entire enterprise to work together, building trust and empowerment throughout the company. What it comes down to is two-way communication.*

And Volvo Rents' CFO is hardly complaining, partly because between 2004 and 2005, business with loyal customers grew by more than 200 percent. It's also because of open lines of communication between the "brand folk" and the "money folk", as well as the resulting quantitative approach the marketing team has adopted.

The key to friendly CMO-CFO relations is a marketing strategy based on real economics: if you ground your plan in economics, theoretically you can do most anything and still keep management happy.

> *In response to a finance department "business plan", the marketing department at Volvo Rents creates its own "customer plan"—a strategy for marketing spending based on the customer database. The "customer plan" quantitatively ties to the company's "business plan."*

For example, currently 10 percent of Volvo Rents' customers account for 83 percent of the company's business and 90 percent plus of profitability. As a result, 90 percent of the marketing budget is devoted to that 10 percent.

Finally, enlist the finance department to analyze the marketing department's customer database. This means that the CFO and the CMO are working with the same data from day one. That's the foundation of good communication.

As a brief recap, setting quantifiable marketing goals that are directly tied to your company's financial goals:

1. Enables your company to plan with a much higher degree of precision, predictability and visibility. This results in greater alignment between all of the functional areas in your company.

2. Allows you to establish a tremendous amount of trust with your CFO.

In the next chapter, you'll find more details on how to segment and manage your customer base in order to better manage your customer portfolio and sales pipeline.

CONTRARIAN
MARK**Ǝ**TING

CHAPTER EIGHT:
CUSTOMER SEGMENTATION & THE SALES PIPELINE

Chapter Eight: Customer Segmentation & the Sales Pipeline

> *"The beaten path is safest, but the traffic is terrible."*
>
> —*Jeff Taylor, Monster.com founder*

In prior sections I've helped you to focus on B-of-B customers that represent a small percentage of your customer base, and a large percentage of your revenue and profitability. Segmenting your customer base lets you easily view your customers based on their relative value to your organization.

I recommend six (6) customer segments for your entire customer base so that you can quickly identify patterns. In addition to B-of-B customers there are five customer segments that will assist you in managing and identifying patterns within your customer relationship pipeline: future B-of-B customers, new customers, recently departed customers, long lost customers and testers.

B-of-B: Customers that are "addicted" to your company's products and services.

Future B-of-B: Customers that have demonstrated a commitment to your company's products or services, but less frequently than B-of-B.

New Customers: Customers that have just begun to transact with your company.

Recently Departed: Former B-of-B customers who have stopped doing business with you.

Long Lost: Previous B-of-B customers who have not transacted in the last six months.

Testers: Customers who have demonstrated little or no commitment to your business.

A brief definition of each:

Best of the Best customers:

B-of-B customers are those that are "addicted" to your company's products and services. They transact recently (in the last 30 days) and frequently. In the context of Volvo Rents, B-of-B customers transact 24+ times per year, and each spend on average $35,000 annually. By using RFM scoring of your customer base, you can identify which customers rely on your products and services for their day-to-day activities. Chances are, you know these customers by name and have adapted your operations to consistently deliver flexible and exceptional customer service to these customers. Keep in mind that RFM score weighting will depend based on what is most predictive within your business.

Future Best of the Best customers:

Future B-of-B customers are those customers that have demonstrated a commitment to your company's products or services, transacting recently (in the last 60 days) but less frequently than B-of-B. With Volvo Rents customers, future B-of-B transact 12-23 times per year.

These customers represent five percent of the customer base and 10 percent of total revenue. Their annual revenue contribution is $8,000 per year (approximately four (4) times less than the B-of-B customers).

Chances are you recognize the faces of these customers, but you have not yet established a personal or name-based connection. *They greatly appreciate your company's products and services but do not have an emotional connection to your company.*

These customers are worth examining, as they have the greatest potential to become your next B-of-B customers. What's necessary is for you to determine if they have the potential to transact with your company more frequently.

Once you have examined each name and validated their potential, it is essential that you establish high-impact tactics that breakthrough to these customers so they know that you value them and are reaching out to develop an emotional connection.

New Customers:

The new customer segment represents those customers that have just begun to transact with your company. This segment has the value of enforcing a discipline upon your organization to (1) evaluate whether these customers might transact again to become either B-of-B or future B-of-B customers and (2) give you a chance to welcome them to your business with a thoughtful welcome gift, a note, or an offer to invoke a second transaction.

Recently Departed:

Recently departed customers are your former B-of-B customers who have stopped doing business with you for some reason. In the next chapter, I will discuss developing an early warning and response system for this segment.

Long Lost:

Long lost customers are previous B-of-B that have not transacted in the last six months. Long lost customers have a recency score of 181-731+ days (meaning they have not transacted with this company for at least six (6) months) and frequency score of 12-23 and 24+. From time to time, you should use this segmentation as a reminder to reach out to these former B-of-B customers and assess whether they are ready and able to do business with your company again.

Testers:

The tester group is often the segmentation in which many businesses go awry. Testers are those customers who have demonstrated little or no commitment to your business. They transact one to five times per year and are price-sensitive. Generally, they constantly compare your prices to the competition and demonstrate NO loyalty to your company. I urge you to be cautious with this group, as they are often extremely high maintenance; asking for service and concessions that vastly exceed their contribution to your company's revenue and profit. As a reference point, testers at Volvo Rents comprise approximately 80 percent of customer base, and only 10 percent of revenue.

These six customer segments enable you to quickly determine the relative value of each customer type to your organization. Given that your time and money are finite, this knowledge provides you the option to proportionately allocate resources to each. And more importantly, they enable your company to design customer support processes that provide exceptional attention to your B-of-B customers—first and foremost.

Simple, rolling, twelve-month graphs with green, yellow and red lights are a highly effective way to monitor changes in the customer base. Sample dashboards (with traffic lights and comments) for each are noted below. Example graphs with conclusions are noted on the following pages.

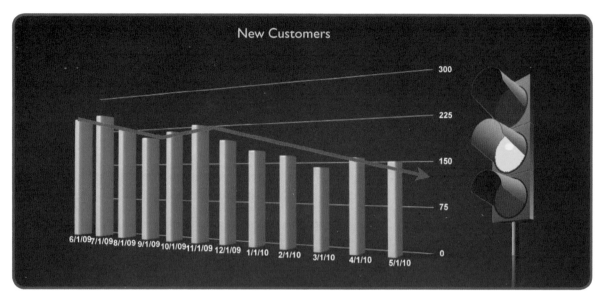

You have 145 new customers, about equal to your average of 176. You should continue your prospecting efforts.

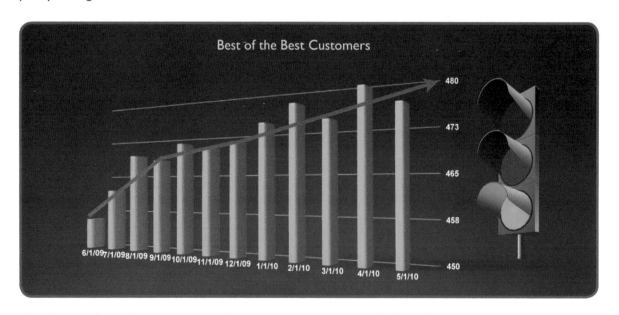

You have 470 B-of-B customers, above your average of 434. Good.

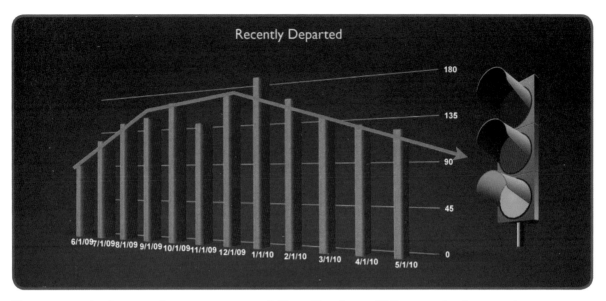

Your recently departed customers are falling. You have 125 recently departed customers, compared with 146 on average. Well done.

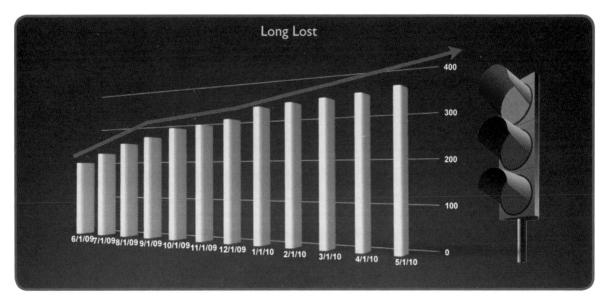

This week's 357 long lost customers exceed your average of 270. Investigate why you are losing them.

By scanning the graphs, you can quickly grasp what is going on with your business before looking at any financial report. You can also draw the following conclusions from these example dashboards:

- **New Customers: yellow light—a cause for concern.** New customers are down substantially from the prior year. Because there is always a natural rate of attrition in your customer base, you need a steady stream of new customers to maintain and grow your business.

- **B-of-B Customers: green light—Fantastic!** While new customers are down, you are maintaining and growing your B-of-B customers vs. the prior year. Since the B-of-B customers drive the majority of your revenue and profits, your business is secure. Continue to focus on adding new B-of-B customers.

- **Recently Departed Customers—over the past six months, 'recently departed' customers have declined substantially.** Your business is doing a very good job in preventing the attrition of your best customers. However, when comparing 'recently departed' customers over the past year, the numbers of 'recently departed' customers are still higher than last year. Examine your customer retention programs for B-of-B customers.

- **Long Lost Customers: this number is alarmingly high for the last 12 months and is trending higher.** This group represents your previous B-of-B customers who had shown tremendous appreciation and affinity for your business. Take a random sampling, and go talk to these customers to find out why they are no longer doing business with you.

These techniques can and do work, as evidenced by an entrepreneur marketing expert who applied them in the real-life workplace:

"The customer dashboard is a great marketing tool. It helps me track my customers on a weekly basis and gives me a snapshot of where we stand with them. The Dashboard Report helps me focus better on our customers," David T., entrepreneur, Rochester, New York

Hertz car rental, among other auto rental companies, utilizes data on premium customers to spotlight their VIP customers, offering them perks that range from Platinum card memberships to guaranteed car availability. One CEO paid $60.00 a year as of 2009 for a "Hertz #1 Club Gold Card," giving him faster check-in and check-out service.

The rationale is that the frequent customer who qualifies for these special perks falls under the **Contrarian Marketing** rule of business—meaning they are the B-of-B customers, and should be handled with special care.

Creating and Managing Your Sales Pipeline:

I am often asked by a wide range of business people what is the "ideal" distribution of a customer base among the six customer segmentations (B-of-B, Future B-of-B, New Customers, Recently Departed, Long Lost, and Testers).

You might be surprised: **there is NO right answer**.

The purpose of customer segmentation is to provide you with a current view and an easy mechanism to understand the relative value of your customer base. **What's most important is that you:**

- **Constantly assess the status of each customer segment.**

- **Set revenue and profitability goals for each segment.**

- **Establish the level of service that you intend to provide to each segment.**

- **Determine the sales and marketing tactics that you aim to use for each segment.**

- **Focus on analyzing and moving each customer set towards the B-of-B segment. Remember: your goal is to capture as much of your customers' potential spending by showering them with the appropriate level of attention and service.**

In the example on the next page, nine percent of the customers generate 85 percent of the company's total revenue. It shows, graphically, the potential of revenue creation by moving customers from right to left—and showering the "right" customers with exceptional attention and service to make them "raving fans."

By looking at the number of customers within each segment, I can quickly arrive at the conclusion that I only need a few more customers in the B-of-B and future B-of-B segments to achieve my revenue goals.

Constantly monitor and set goals for the number of B-of-B and future B-of-B customers that your business requires to achieve its growth goals.

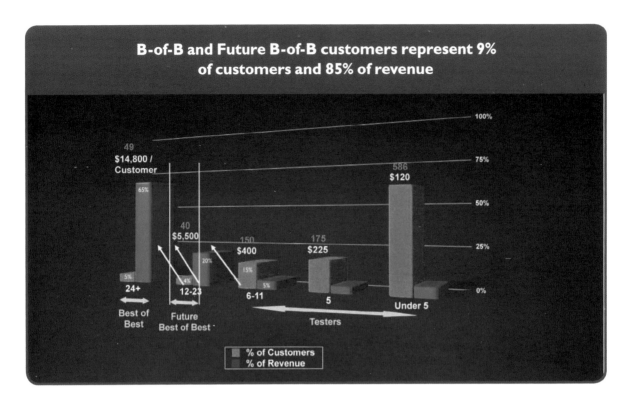

The ideal sales pipeline is a linear pyramid: from bottom to top, you should have the fewest number of VIP customers at the top of the pyramid, with the goal of moving customers up to higher and higher levels, until they become B-of-B customers.

Below is an example of a sales pyramid based on the same data as that which is presented above:

CLIMBING THE PYRAMID TO MARKETING SUCCESS
(# Of Customers)

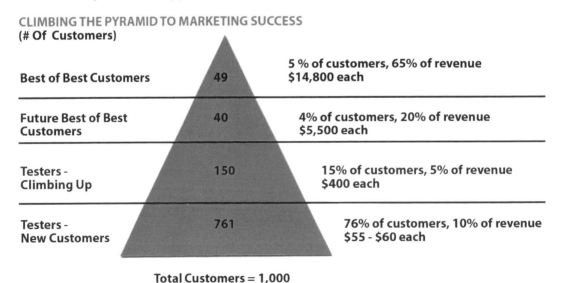

Best of Best Customers	49	5 % of customers, 65% of revenue $14,800 each
Future Best of Best Customers	40	4% of customers, 20% of revenue $5,500 each
Testers - Climbing Up	150	15% of customers, 5% of revenue $400 each
Testers - New Customers	761	76% of customers, 10% of revenue $55 - $60 each

Total Customers = 1,000

Where do you see opportunity to grow the example customer base?

This business has achieved remarkable success in nurturing and growing their success with their B-of-B customers. They now have 49 B-of-B customers spending almost three times what the future B-of-B customers spend. They should continue to focus on growing this segment to multiply their success.

In order to maximize their efforts in growing the B-of-B segment, the business should focus on having a greater number of future B-of-B customers.

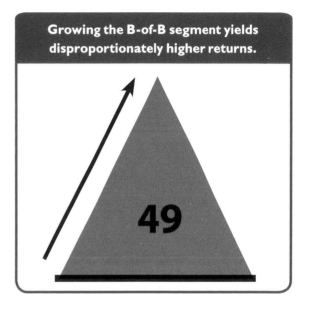

Growing the B-of-B segment yields disproportionately higher returns.

Since they have fewer future B-of-B customers (40 customers) than B-of-B customers (49 customers) the rate of growth may slow because there are less customers to work with in grooming them to move to the next level of customer loyalty.

Now that we've looked at ways to manage your data, and showed you what to expect from your tiered layer of customers, let's examine ways to spot those "dangerous" renegades who can kill a business - your Recently Departed customers.

They are former B-of-B customers who, for some reason or another, have "high-tailed" it out of town. Your job is to find out why, and what to do about it.

> *In a perfect world, moving from the top of the sales pyramid down, each layer should have more customers than the one above it. The sales pyramid enables management to quickly view the business's strengths, its opportunities and rate of growth.*

CONTRARIAN
MARKƎTING

CHAPTER NINE:
FIVE ALARM FIRE-DEVELOPING AN EARLY WARNING & RESPONSE SYSTEM FOR RECENTLY DEPARTED CUSTOMERS

Chapter 9: Five Alarm Fire - Developing an Early Warning and Response System for Recently Departed Customers

> *"To not prepare is the greatest of crimes; to be prepared beforehand for any contingency is the greatest of virtues."*
>
> —*Sun Tzu, Art of War*

Recently departed customers are often your former B-of-B that have stopped doing business with you for some reason. **This is a five-alarm fire and you should immediately investigate the reason.** Since B-of-B customers are the platform of your business's profitability and growth, the loss of a few of these customers could have a major impact on your business.

Generally, the reasons could be one of the following:

1. **Business conditions or needs have changed, and they no longer require your products or service.**

2. **A competitor has predatorily recruited one of your B-of-B customers away from you.**

3. **You have dropped the ball and lost the customer for some reason - dissatisfaction with your service or the fact that they feel under-appreciated by you.**

4. **The market for your company's products or services is fundamentally changing- analyzing lost customers vs. industry market share is a good indicator of whether your problem is internal or industry related. A signal of an industry related problem is when you are losing customers but your market share remains constant.**

Developing an early warning and response system for 'recently departed' customers is a fairly easy task. By monitoring your 'recently departed' on a weekly basis, you should realize right away that there is a problem.

Developing an early warning and response system for 'recently departed' customers is a fairly easy task. By monitoring your 'recently departed' on a weekly basis, you should realize right away that there is a problem. Quick outreach to these customers will provide you with invaluable insight as to why they departed, and give you the opportunity to reignite customer loyalty.

> *Customers whose behavior with you is changing (either accelerating or terminating) indicates an important marketing opportunity. Here is where the marketing dollar has the most leverage.*
> *—Ronald C. Goodstein, Ph.D.*

Management and the salesperson together can develop a short check-list:

(1) Research your company's performance on the account:

a. Have you consistently treated this customer as a VIP?

b. Is your competition out-performing you? How, where, why?

   i. What can you do to out-perform your competition?

c. What can you improve?

(2) Research this company's market performance:

a. Are they successful and growing? If not, your **recently departed** dashboard may be signaling a material change to this company's business. Watch the credit that you extend to this customer and develop a plan to collect your accounts receivable exposure with this client.

(3) Your CEO or senior management should accompany the sales person in visiting the **recently departed**. The loss of a great customer provides a terrific learning opportunity on ways to win them back. In addition, you can:

a. Understand your company's view of itself vs. your customer's view of your company.

b. Gain valuable knowledge on the economy and market: is it growing, softening or contracting?

c. Gain valuable knowledge on your competitors – their strengths and weaknesses.

If the **recently departed** customers left your company because you failed in some fashion, this customer is seeking immediate recognition of the problem and resolution. Take this opportunity to "wow" the customer and bring them back with your honesty and commitment. You may have to make meaningful concessions, but the price of losing the life-time value of one of your B-of-B customers will make any concession worthwhile. In fact, early research revealed that successful service recovery led to the anomalous outcome of better customer loyalty relative to the loyalty evidenced by customers that never had a service failure at all (Hart, Christopher W.L., James L. Heskett, and W. Earl Sasser, Jr. (1990), "The Profitable Art of Service Recovery," *Harvard Business Review*, July-August, 148-156). Often just an acknowledgment and apology is enough to win a customer back.

> *Not all customers are created equal, and neither are the reasons they leave you.*

In my experience, customers will tell you what you are doing right and where you are going wrong. If they don't, ask them, and do it often. To them, a brand is only as good as their *most recent encounter.*

Remember: Not all customers are created equal and neither are the reasons they leave you. Customer defection analysis is key to the retention of B-of-B customers that are still in the fold and worthwhile, even if service recovery strategies do not win-back the specific client that you lost. As Reichfeld and Sasser suggested more than a decade ago, "To learn how to keep customers, track the ones you lose." ("Zero Defections: Quality Comes to Services," *Harvard Business Review*, September-October, 105-111).

Your next challenge is to craft the customer experience that will serve as your marketing platform, enabling you to retain B-of-B customers and attract new B-of-B customers. Your customer experience should be centered on a key concept: the lifetime value of B-of-B customers to your business. That's our next chapter.

CONTRARIAN MARKΞTING

CHAPTER TEN:
CUSTOMER EXPERIENCE & LIFETIME VALUE–
PROMISE v. EXPECTATIONS

Chapter 10: Customer Experience & Lifetime Value - Promise v. Expectations

> *"Someone's sitting in the shade today because someone planted a tree a long time ago."*
>
> —Warren Buffet, investor

Customer Lifetime Value (CLV) is defined as the net present value of future cash flows attributed to a customer. Put more simply, CLV is the dollar value of the customer relationship to the firm. The difference between Customer Profit and CLV is that profit measures the past and CLV attempts to measure the future. While both are useful in shaping a manager's decisions, quantifying CLV involves forecasting future activities.

Ask yourself what your company is willing to pay to acquire a customer relationship, and what it would be willing to pay to avoid losing a customer relationship. If you consider such relationships an asset, CLV represents the dollar value.

But how do you go about creating a customer relationship, one that establishes lifetime value? It all comes down to two things: Promise and Expectation.

In 2007, American Express CEO, Kenneth Chenault, made a profound speech to the Economic Club of Washington, D.C. In a nutshell, he said the essential outcome of any marketing and sales tactic must involve knowing what the customer expects and ensuring that the company delivers.

"From the consumer's perspective, a particular brand creates an expectation. From the company's perspective it creates a promise."
–Kenneth Chenault, CEO, American Express

"From the consumer's perspective," he said, "a particular brand creates an expectation. From the company's perspective it creates a promise. Without these mutually reinforcing perspectives, a company would start from zero each and every day. And that's no way to run a business."

Chenault went on to say that if a company wanted to stay in business, it had to have integrity. Strong brands are built steadily through day-to-day actions, he said, and by consistently meeting a customer's expectations.

He asked the audience to think about some of the most recognized customer brands to date -- Starbucks, Amazon, Virgin, Costco, all well-known companies that still evoke a strong image. Costco, for example, conjures an image of value; Starbucks with a premium customer experience. You do not see commercials for Costco or billboards for Amazon, and yet each of these brands resonates with us as customers.

Applied to your own business, it is essential that four things happen:

1. You develop a customer-based USP that resonates with customers (the Promise).

2. Your marketing and sales teams must constantly deliver the 'promise' (or USP) based on your customers' expectations.

3. Your marketing and sales teams must constantly remind your customers that you have delivered on that promise.

4. Your operations team must deliver the experience that your marketing and sales teams have promised.

Amercian Express CEO, Kenneth Chenault, asks one "to think about some of the most recognized consumer brands to date --Starbucks, Amazon, Virgin, Costco, all well-known companies that evoke a strong image."

United Airlines learned the hard way what happens when you fail to follow through on a brand name that promises much but delivers inconsistently. In what may have been an isolated incident, at least in the customer's mind, the company chose to cut costs at the expense of good loyal customers who expected more from a brand they had learned to trust through the years.

Guitarist Dave Carroll was in a window seat waiting for a United plane to take off from Chicago's O'Hare airport. Looking out, he spotted baggage handlers literally hurling guitar cases through the air. When he complained to the flight attendants, they appeared indifferent. Arriving at his destination, he found -- not surprisingly -- that his prized guitar was smashed (*Forbes.com*, "United Airlines Shows How Not to Run Your Business," by Shawn Rein, 7/24/09).

Months of complaining to the airline followed, to no avail. So he wrote and performed a song about his unhappy experience with United, posted it on YouTube, and had more than three million hits in the first ten days.

Like many companies in these circumstances, United may have gotten bogged down in focusing only on sustaining its operations. *They forgot they were selling more than a means of fast transportation (functional benefits) when what they were really selling were the hopes and dreams of countless vacationers and others who had a vested interest in the memory of a brand they once saw as representative of the glamorous world of flying high (emotional benefits).* That is, the company had violated its promise of emotional benefits in order to standardize its functional ones.

By contrast, winning companies like Disney and Apple Computer go out of their way to create brand loyalty and lifetime customer value, not just attempt to meet minimum standards for customer satisfaction.

A trip to Disney World, for example, is an experience in the creation of lifelong memories. Their employees at all levels are trained as "dream weavers" selling not just a product, but

A trip to Disney World is an experience in the creation of lifelong memories. Their employees at all levels are trained as "dream weavers", selling not just a product, but an experience.

an experience. **Walt Disney realized that this was no easy task, "There is no magic to magic. It is all in the details."** The same is true at Apple, where customers not only spend more, they become "brand ambassadors" and bring other customers along.

With average customers more price sensitive today than ever before, they refuse to waste money on brands that do not meet their expectations. They will buy what they trust, and they will return to trusted brands over and over.

Companies that recognize this, and offer more than basic functionality, will continue to thrive (*Forbes.com*, 7/24/09). And they will continue to match their promises to their customers' expectations. It really is that simple! *In his pioneering book, Managing Brand Equity, brand guru David A. Aaker suggests that strong brands are those that make clear promises and keep them over time, whereas weak brands often continually change their promises and/or fail to consistently deliver upon them (Managing Brand Equity, Free Press, 1991).* Establishing your "promise" statement will enable your company and employees to stay focused on what you are trying to accomplish. Once you've defined your market positioning, you can begin to envision the type of experience you need to create with your B-of-B customers to deliver on this promise.

Creating the Right Experience for Your B-of-B.

In 1998, Joseph Pines and James H. Gilmore, two business gurus who led the way in announcing the arrival of a new era in marketing, published their landmark book: *The Experience Economy.* They explained that modern marketing strategies have changed from selling products and services to selling customer *experiences.* Starbucks is doing just that, which is one of the reasons they are now an American icon.

Pine and Gilmore explained that modern marketing strategies have changed from selling products and services to selling customer experiences. Starbucks is doing just that, which is one of the reasons they are now an American icon.

Consider your cup of morning coffee. It takes about three cents worth of beans to make coffee at home. You pay a dollar or so to have it served at your local diner. At Starbucks you pay about $2.00 to $4.00 a cup. One of the great success stories of the 21st century, Starbucks grew from a single store in Seattle, WA, more than 30 years ago, to nearly 2400 stores in 28 countries. By fiscal year 2009, the company was posting revenues of $9.8 billion (Indiana University Kelley School of Business, *Business Horizons*, 2005, pg. 433; www.wsj.com 2010).

What led to their phenomenal success was more than just a good cup of coffee. It was their genius in turning a pedestrian commodity (coffee) into a pleasant life experience. Today, Starbucks is known as a social gathering place for students and young professionals. Pine and Gilmore contend that the USA is fast becoming "an experience economy" in which all successful businesses must sell an experience; an economy where we turn our businesses into theatrical stages for an experience to occur.

Apple's vision was to make the customer experience tactile, fun and memorable.

Courtesy of Apple

Apple Computer, Inc. followed this advice by offering the "Apple Store Experience," with targeted customers in mind. Their vision was to make the customer experience tactile, fun and memorable; one that would carry through in revenue growth.

Unlike traditional retailers who categorize by product line, Apple was among the first to arrange its products in ways in which customers actually use them. For example, when a customer looks for a digital camera or a photo printer, all accompanying software is easily accessible. Professional consultants are available to help answer questions and provide hands-on demonstrations, from how to burn a CD to how to publish a photo. Online games can be played onsite and some Apple stores have multimedia theatres to enhance the overall customer "experience."

Starwood Hotels and Resorts, parent company of W and Westin Hotels (referenced in Chapter One as Case Study #3), has about 980 properties in nearly 100 countries. Last year, they launched

In his pioneering book Managing Brand Equity, brand guru David A. Aaker suggests that strong brands are those that make clear promises and keep them over time, whereas weak brands often continually change their promises and/or fail to consistently deliver upon them (Managing Brand Equity, Free Press, 1991).

a pilot "customer experience management program" in order to go one step beyond traditional frequent-guest marketing models. From "Heavenly Beds" to localized fashion shows for select female guests, Starwood is reinventing the hotel experience. Starwood members are assigned a single point of contact, called a Starwood Ambassador, whose sole purpose is to take care of each guest in a special and meaningful way. The extra emphasis on enhancing the customer's experience worked, for Starwood plans to expand the program in 2010 (*Hospitality Design*, "Brand Identity," No. 1, July 2010).

Case Study #5: Chipotle Creates Human Experience that Brings Long-term Value: As of 2009, Chipotle Mexican Grill, Inc. owned and operated more than 956 casual quick-service establishments in 35 states (mostly urban areas) and was known for its burritos and other Mexican foods. It appealed to young adults who preferred made-to-order items featuring organically-grown produce and grew its loyal customer base with a simple philosophy: food served fast doesn't have to be a "fast-food" experience.

Chipotle has grown its loyal customer base with a simple philosophy: food served fast doesn't have to be a "fast-food" experience.

Founder Steven Ells, who is chairman and CEO of Denver-based Chipotle, says his company's marketing has always been based on the belief that the best and most recognizable brands aren't built through advertising or promotional campaigns alone. He calls traditional advertising "not believable" and says his company spends less on ads in one year than rival McDonald's spends in 48 hours (*Business Week*, July 13, 2010).

While most fast food chains bombard customers with mass media commercials to herald their latest menu item, the Mexican chain depends on <u>customers</u> to spread the word. This all-volunteer army does its job well, generating word-of-mouth advertising that keeps Chipotle growing. They expected to open between 120 – 130 new restaurants in 2010.

> *According to Steven Ellis, Chipotle spends less on ads in one year than rival McDonald's spends in 48 hours.*

Free samples are also part of the Chipotle marketing strategy. When its new establishment opened in Manhattan in July 2009, the company gave away burritos to 6,000 people, many of whom stood in line for hours. The cost was $6,000, but the company landed 6,000 new customers – and 6,000 spokespeople that will likely continue to carry their message forward.

Lifetime Value Mind over Matter

A lifetime value mind-set is an essential concept to long-term profitability. Consider these two scenarios:

1. Reactive: if a B-of-B customer has a problem with your service, under which mind-set would you be more willing to resolve their problem?

   a. Transaction mind-set: The customer wants to return your $500 product after using the item consistently for the last 60 days or:

   b. Lifetime value mind-set: The customer wants to return your $500 product after using the item consistently for the last 60 days - - but you know that they spend $10,000 annually and have spent $50,000 over their life-time with your business. Under which scenario would you act and accommodate the customer so that they continue to do business with you over their lifetime?

2. Proactive: if you are trying to earn a B-of-B prospect's business whom you know spends $100,000 annually with your competition, under which mind-set would you be more willing to accommodate an unusual request:

   a. Transaction mind-set: The customer asks to use your product or service for FREE for 90 days – (a $10,000 value and $5,000 cost to you) since they already have a vested relationship with your competitor or:

   b. Lifetime value mind-set: Knowing that the customer has the potential to spend $100,000 with you annually and be a profitable account, you enthusiastically say 'yes' to this unusual request, because you know that this opportunity gives you permission to establish a close relationship with the prospect over the next 90 days. You agree to this opportunity with the caveat that the prospect agrees to meet with you weekly for progress / assessment updates.

Can you commit to offering a premium service and product, consistently to your B-of-B customers and prospects? Can you design your functional departments - operations, sales, customer support, accounting, etc. - so that they can flexibly adapt to the needs of B-of-B customers? I believe you can.

For a helpful diagram in identifying and managing customer touchpoints by functional department, refer to to the Contrarian Marketing Process Diagrams **in the Appendix**.

If you consider that a few customers will generate the majority of your revenue and profit, it's easy to consistently accommodate them. Before you know it, you'll have an army of "raving fan" customers – people that won't desert you.

Stew Leonard Sees the Big Picture

In Connecticut, the popular grocery store Stew Leonard's has a lifetime value mindset. Leonard spoke to one of my college classes at the University of Michigan in 1990. He said that when he sees a customer walking through the door, he does not see her as a mother buying a $3.00 gallon of milk. Instead, he visualizes her based on her annual value to his business – a $10,000 per year customer who consistently spends $200 per week at his store.

Structuring your marketing strategy around the lifetime value mind-set will lead you to craft marketing tactics that end with recent and frequent interactions with your B-of-B customers. The result: premium brands are not only able to command a premium price, but serve as an essential protective barrier that will keep your competition away from your B-of-B customers.

How does this apply to your business in retaining customers? Your office, store, company vehicles and sales people are your stage to engineer the customer experience

> **Stew Leonard built a highly successful grocery store in Connecticut through a lifetime value mind-set.**
>
> **"Rule #1, the customer is always right. Rule #2, if the customer is ever wrong, see Rule #1".**
> **- Stew Leonard**

for your B-of-B customers. All you must do is set the stage to create the experience that the customer is seeking. While this varies industry-to-industry, we know from customer research and human psychology that B-of-B customers desire the experience of being:

- Significant
- Appreciated
- Liked
- Important

Is your business doing all that it can to ensure that each of your B-of-B customers feel significant, appreciated, liked and important?

> *Engaging the customer's five senses will facilitate your success in making your customers feel significant, appreciated, liked and important.*

If so, try to figure out why your B-of-B customers like your business on an emotional level. Once you understand *why* they like you, all you have to do is 'play' their emotional experience back to them on the 'stage' that they envision.

Pine and Gilmore say that leading-edge companies are finding the next higher level value in experiences that occur when a company *uses services as a stage*, with goods as props, in order to create a memorable event.

Specifically, they convey that engaging the customer's five senses (sight, sound, touch, smell and taste) will facilitate your success in making your customers feel significant, appreciated, liked and important.

Volvo Rents Engages Customers

Here is an example from Volvo of how to ensure that every experience is intrinsically sensory by engaging the customers' five senses:

- **Sight:** We have signs throughout Volvo Rents locations that convey flexibility and approachability: 'Welcome to the Friendliest Rental Store in Town'.

- **Sound:** We have sound systems outside and inside our stores where we play our customers' favorite music. We concentrate on using sound when we greet and personally welcome our B-of-B customers by name.

- **Touch:** We use touch when we shake their hands as they enter our stores or when we visit them on job sites.

- **Smell:** We employ the tantalizing smell of popcorn, coffee and cookies inside the 'contractor's corner' in the retail showroom of our stores.

- **Taste:** Foods our customers enjoy don't just smell good; they taste good. Along with a pleasant taste comes a pleasant memory of where that food came from.

When Getting Your Foot in the Door is Problematic.

It's just as true in business as in other aspects of your life: some relationships are harder to build and maintain than others.

A local store owner called me with a problem. He had significant opportunities with local businesses that would not allow him or his salesmen "through their door." All their defenses were up.

With great assistance from the marketing department, a customer acquisition campaign was crafted to target high-stakes prospects. Co-owners of the operation compiled a detailed list with the help of *their* sales team. The list profiled each customer, what was known about both the prospect (personally and professionally) and the company that currently served their needs.

The list was tremendously helpful in crafting a suitable USP and marketing plan to each prospect not just for the marketing department. The sales staff learned important details that would later help establish a good working relationship.

With list in hand, marketing produced a premium gift package that contained company branded Grade-A quality gourmet food and other company specific items, from bumper stickers to a custom, hand-signed note addressed to each prospect. All items (costs averaged $10 - $40 per item) were packed in the special company-branded gift box. The gifts were then mailed directly to the prospects' office within four days of the gift order being placed, and followed up with a phone call from the general manager.

Feedback was positive.

"We were very pleased with the response," the store owner reported. "These people wouldn't even take a call from us before getting the gift. One person called to say they appreciated the gift and would be talking to me soon about sending us some business. Another prospect of a large company called to talk about doing business together, this time before I had a chance to place a follow-up call."

He also reported that the secretaries received some of the food, so there was added goodwill. He was now halfway through the two-step marketing strategy.

In the next chapter you'll learn how to expand these and other marketing techniques in order to ensure that you not only build a great customer relationship in the short term, but that you create a customer base through the right culture that flourishes and lasts.

CONTRARIAN
MARK3TING

CHAPTER ELEVEN:
HOW TO BUILD & MAINTAIN THE RIGHT CULTURE

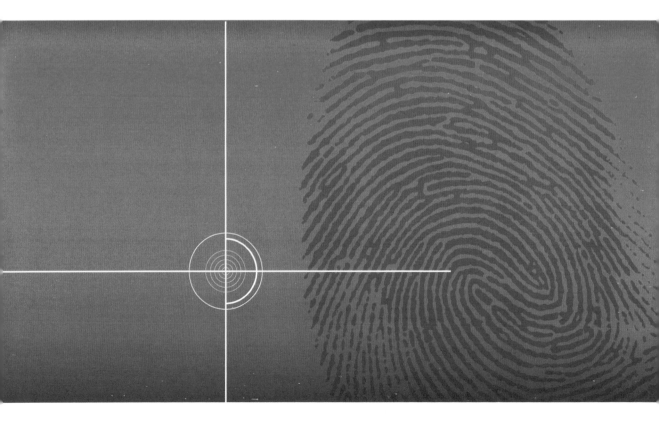

Chapter Eleven: How to Build & Maintain the Right Culture

> *"Should you find yourself in a chronically leaky boat, energy devoted to changing vessels is more productive than energy devoted to patching leaks."*
>
> —*Warren Buffett, investor*

Have you ever wondered why some businesses have extended track records of success through every stage of growth - - from small to large? Conversely, have you ever noticed that many companies fail when transitioning from a successful small or mid-size firm to a large company?

In 1998 I met a business owner, Don O'Neal, whose construction and industrial equipment rental company offered the best customer service environment that I had ever experienced. Better customer service than Nordstrom, better than the Ritz-Carlton - you name the company – and then multiply by two. Every employee was universally pleasant and enthusiastic about his/her work.

Interestingly, Don's company had more than 50 percent margins in Earnings before Interest, Taxes, Depreciation, and Amortization, or EBITDA vs. the norm EBITDA margin of 20-35 percent for the rest of the industry. Don was highly regarded as having one of the best companies in the history of the $35+ billion construction equipment rental industry.

I asked many of Don's employees: "To what do you attribute your success?" The response was identical every time – "Taking care of the customer."

Fresh out of business school a few years earlier at UCLA's Anderson Graduate School of Management, I regarded the concept of "culture" in business as a "pop" business concept conceived to make consultants money and give employees a distraction when not working. *What was Don's secret?*

Don and his family, among the finest business leaders I have ever met, invested themselves in applying Christian values to create a culture of respect and nourishment for their employees. The result: an enterprise where every employee prided themselves in going the extra mile to 'take care of the customer.'

Don also offered me a book, *The Way of the Shepherd, Seven Ancient Secrets to Managing Productive People* by Dr. Kevin Leman and William Pentak that opened my eyes into best ways to develop the right culture. I encourage you to read it if you are searching for how to develop and sustain your company's culture.

Paul Bullock, Volvo Rents Franchise of the Year Winner multiple times, calls it a little book that packs a big message and is an inspiring lesson in leadership:

"Everybody in my company is very customer-service oriented. The customer is first and foremost. We are only as good as the employees that surround us. If we are taking good care of our employees and they in turn are taking good care of our customers - which is ultimately going to grow our business - more customers will flock through our door. I highly recommend this book to anyone who manages people."

Bullock has put *The Way of the Shepherd* principles to work in a big way. We talk consistently about the book in management meetings and sales meetings. It bears repeating that business is not just about taking care of the customer; you also have to take care of your own.

Building the Culture

> *While consumer goods are sold to mass markets, business-to-business (B2B) products and services are increasingly developed in close interaction with specialized customers, involving many separate functions within both the seller and buyer organizations. This implies that while consumer brands are mass marketed by the marketing department and extensively promoted through advertising and public relations, B2B brands are driven by personal interactions. It is the people within the organization, their skills, values, attitudes and behavior – the corporate culture – that give substance to the brand and credibility to the company.*
>
> *– The Volvo Group – Brand Management*

Some may still dismiss the concepts of "culture", "mission", "vision" and "wanted position" as pop-business speak or new age concepts, but I would argue the contrary.

Development and commitment to culture within a company has many historical examples of success in business: Intel (Andy Grove, former CEO, has written several books on the subject), Volvo (the Volvo Way), BMW, Virgin Atlantic, Apple, Nordstrom, Southwest Airlines, and American Express, all believe in the power of relationship-building internally and externally.

A culture is a set of beliefs, usually established by the founder of the company, about how employees should behave when:

- Positively interacting with each other: allowing individual independence and empowerment, while staying rooted to a team concept.

- Interacting with customers and establishing a vision of the customer experience.

- Interacting with suppliers.

- Performing the tasks of their day-to-day jobs.

- Interacting with superiors, peers and subordinates.

- Adapting and customizing the business model to each and every market (while staying true to the company's core values).

- Establishing guidelines about how the corporate office interacts with field offices and field employees.

As an example, for over 200 years the "Volvo Way" has been instrumental in helping the Volvo Group to:

a. Maintain the heritage of its founders and their core beliefs of "caring for the passenger / operator more than any other transport company."

b. Maintain a commitment to its core values of quality, safety and care for the environment.

c. Continue to grow a successful, global enterprise with over 100,000 employees on all seven continents.

> **Key ideas include:**
>
> **Mission, Vision and Wanted Position:**
>
> The **Mission Statement** detailing your business concept – your reason for being.
>
> The **Vision** explaining your ultimate objective – where you are going and how you want to be perceived in the future.
>
> **Wanted Position** is the list of specific long-term objectives that define the right place for your company.

Volvo is good example of a company that has built a unique, long-standing culture around the "Volvo Way." That means interacting with customers and creating a positive customer experience while maintaining quality, safety and care for the environment. All are part of Volvo's core values.

Corporate values: as an example, Volvo's core values are quality, safety and care for the environment.

Building the culture:
Employees: developing individuals to focus on "energy, passion and respect for individuals."

Instructing employees about a standard of behavior:

- Customer focus
- Continual improvements
- Open dialogue
- Clear objectives
- Feedback and follow-up
- Company spirit
- Utilizing common strengths
- Teamwork
- Leadership

Building the Culture: Volvo works towards developing individuals to focus on "energy, passon and respect for individuals" as well as instructing employees about a standard of behavior.

Moving from word to action:
By working toward an open decision-making process, we strive to attain personal commitment to our objectives. To be involved and empowered in setting the direction also means taking individual responsibility and ownership for decisions.

Once a decision has been made, we focus on implementation. We must be able to execute – proceed from word to action – and change faster than our competitors. Otherwise, someone else will take the lead (Source: *The Volvo Way*).

Moving from word to effective action requires the ability to:

Quantify - Quantify means determining if actions that we take, or plan to take, are appropriate and effective.

Measure - When deciding on an action, we need sufficient methods to measure expected results. Measurable results provide goals for our deliveries.

Deliver - Profitability and execution through leadership and customer satisfaction represent the guiding beacons of our operations.

The end result is that your company's culture becomes a living, sustainable, continuous feedback loop that enables your company to adapt to changing market conditions while being grounded to your company's brand heritage of making and keeping a promise to your customer.

Ritz-Carlton Does What It Takes

Employee training is a hallmark of the award winning Ritz-Carlton, a leading brand in luxury lodging. Its unique culture begins with a simple motto: *We are ladies and gentlemen serving ladies and gentlemen.*

Among its unusual policies as of 2009 is allowing each employee to spend up to $2,000 to keep guests happy. No approval from the general manager is required, and the amount is *per incident*, not per year.

Examples include hiring a carpenter to build a shoe tree; setting up special accommodations on the beach (with a newly built walkway) for a handicapped guest; personally returning clothing items left behind even when it means an employee flying halfway across the country to make the delivery.

The idea is to do whatever it takes to create a meaningful experience for a Ritz-Carlton guest. It is, in the words of Simon F. Cooper, hotel president, "about a 'wow story,' which means talking about great things that the employees have done. That is a wonderful training and communication tool, where every department layers on the department message, everywhere, every day" (*Forbes.com*, by R. Reiss, "How Ritz-Carlton Stays on Top," 10/30/09).

The Ritz Carlton allows each employee to spend up to $2,000 per incident to keep guests happy.

Corporate cultures are built on trust – trust among management, among customers, and among the staff that deliver your product or services to the client.

But how do you reach that special B-of-B customer to maximize their long-term value? We explore how in the next chapter.

> *Corporate cultures are built on trust - trust among management, among customers, and among the staff that deliver your product or services to the client.*

CONTRARIAN
MARK∃TING

CHAPTER TWELVE:
MAXIMIZING LIFETIME VALUE OF YOUR
"BEST-OF-BEST" CUSTOMERS

Chapter 12: Maximizing Lifetime Value of Your "Best-of-Best" Customers

> *"In the modern world of business it is useless to be a creative original thinker unless you can also sell what you create."*
>
> —*David M. Ogilvy, British pioneer executive known as the "father of advertising"*

For each B-of-B customer, you can craft a simple marketing calendar that imposes a discipline of marketing to that customer every month or every quarter for years to come.

For example, over twelve months, pick a monthly marketing tactic that is effective in reaching your B-of-B customers and prospects, establish a price for the tactic, and schedule its launch date on your calendar.

Several marketing tactics have shown repeatable success in breaking-through with B-of-B Volvo Rents customers that each spend $35,000 per year.

Below is a copy of a marketing calendar that I have used to target B-of-B customers and prospects, providing tangible rewards for their ongoing customer loyalty.

- **March:** mail a $50 tin of gourmet popcorn or $50 Omaha Steaks gift package with a personalized note as in 'Dear Joe, I hope this note finds you well. As a family-owned business, we greatly appreciate the opportunity to work for you. We hold ourselves to a very high standard in supporting our B-of-B customers and are here for you 24/7. I look forward to visiting soon. Regards, Nick.' The goal is to appear thoughtful and approachable, while engaging your customer's sense of 'taste'.

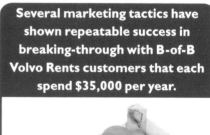

Several marketing tactics have shown repeatable success in breaking-through with B-of-B Volvo Rents customers that each spend $35,000 per year.

- **May:** hand-deliver a large seasonal item (examples: a case of premium Florida citrus or a seasonal item from the Harry & David catalog) with a personalized note. ($25 / person).

- **June**: host a 'lunch and learn' at your customer's facility to learn more about their needs. Invite all of their employees to attend. Bring in a gourmet BBQ lunch for their staff ($15 / person).

- **July:** mail a $10 tin of gourmet Virginia peanuts with a personalized note.

- **September**: mail a note and an ink-jet paper bag that asks your customers to participate in a Thanksgiving food drive for needy families in your area. ($5 / person).

- **October:** invite your customers to your local comedy venue (Improv, etc.) to enjoy a free comedy show that also serves as a fundraiser for the local food bank. ($40 / person).

- **December:** hand-deliver home-made cookies or other home-made items, with a personalized note signed by you and your family. ($15 / person).

The above campaign costs a total of $160 per customer / prospect over the course of the year, and its impact is priceless in humanizing your company. While time intensive, the marketing tactics demonstrate gratitude (March, May, and July), sincere interest in your client's success (June), community involvement and philanthropy (September, October), and gratitude / empathy (December).

Philanthropy: Low-Cost Tactics that Humanize Your Company to Best of Best Customers

A successful philanthropic campaign extends well beyond a goodwill gesture. It can also motivate others to support your company's favorite cause, while exposing them to your brand's core values.

For instance, in 2008, I created the "Hardhat Comedy Tour," inviting customers and/or unemployed construction contractors to attend a show utilizing local talents. The company found that contractors were among the hardest hit during the 2008-09 recession and needed some comic relief aimed at those enduring tough times. Admission was free with the donation of at least three non-perishable foods. Proceeds went to local food banks.

Volvo Rents 'Color for a Cause' community service project, in Atlanta, Georgia, to support Breast Cancer Awareness.

Using this contrarian approach, the company spent about $100,000 to stage 15 events throughout their marketed region, but attracted thousands of "best" customers, and generated over $2 million of public relations exposure on TV, radio, in newspapers, and the Internet. More importantly, a large number of people in need were fed, while the company garnered positive publicity and made a true community connection.

A successful philanthropic campaign extends well beyond a goodwill gesture. It can also motivate others to support your favorite cause while exposing them to your brand's core values.

In addition, Volvo Rents founded the "Color for Cause" campaign in which local stores paint large construction pieces in the color of their favorite charity – for example *pink* to support Breast Cancer Awareness. A portion of the proceeds from renting the equipment are donated to support breast cancer research. In addition, a physically imposing pink Volvo excavator captures customer attention, promotes our brand personality, and invites customers to form a relationship in support of a good cause.

Another low-cost, philanthropic approach is try a brown bag lunch initiative for a local food drive or a Toys for Tots program during the holidays, both of which encourage interaction and deliver the message that your company cares about the community.

> ***Finding your brand voice is a process and must be customized to work best for you and the message you want to relay.***

Include your philanthropic message on everything the customer or prospect sees, from business cards to invoices and e-mail signatures. A typical tag line: 'A portion of our revenue goes to support....' *Make sure this stands out on every form of communication.*

All of these tactics focus on relationship-building - learning exactly what is needed to ensure that your B-of-B customers see you in the best possible light and remain raving fans. Finding your brand voice is a process and must be customized to work best for you and the message you want to relay. As the components come together successfully, the result is a buzz about your brand that will emotionally resonate with your targeted markets.

In the next chapter, I'll share a few secrets that will strengthen your sales and marketing team methods so that your combined efforts reap even more effective results.

CONTRARIAN
MARKETING

CHAPTER THIRTEEN:
TEACHING FIELD EMPLOYEES FORCE MULTIPLICATION

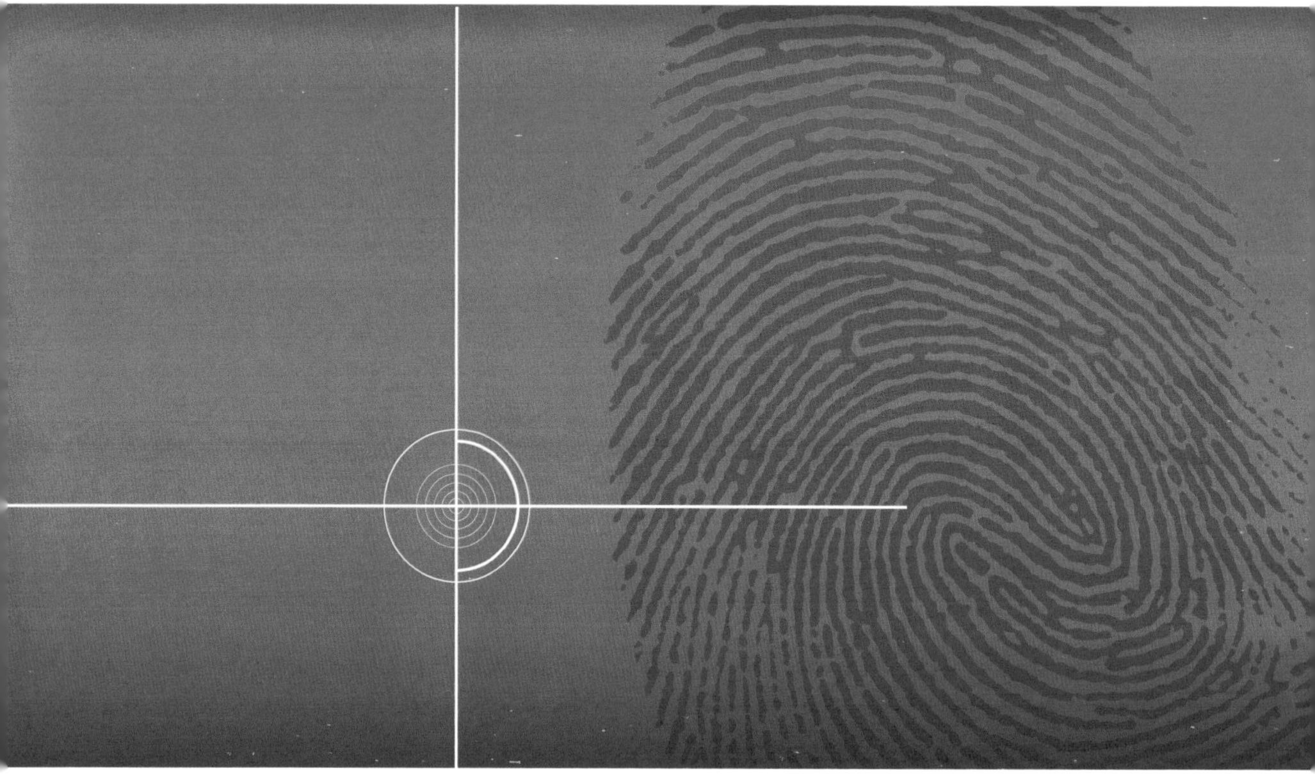

Chapter 13: Teaching Field Employees Force Multiplication

> *"To succeed as a team is to hold all of the members*
>
> *accountable for their expertise."*
>
> —Mitchell Caplan, CEO E*Trade Group Inc.

In many companies, I've observed that the marketing and sales teams don't play well together. In fact, they frequently have an adversarial relationship. This separation is understandable: marketing organizations tend to be more cerebral and passive - - nudging customers to take action. In western terms, they are the ranch-hand cowboys who work hard to keep the place running smooth. The sales organizations are the gun-toting sheriff and deputies that take a stand in front of the customer, daring them to action. Oftentimes, the conflict originates from the sales organization contending that the marketing team does not customize their offering for local markets. And conversely, the marketing organization tends to feel that the sales organization lacks structure and discipline.

"Marketing blames the sales force for its poor execution of an otherwise brilliant rollout plan," said author Dr. Philip Kotler, Distinguished Professor of International Marketing at Northwestern University in Chicago. He and fellow writers, Neil Rackman and Suj Krishnaswamy, explained in a *Harvard Business Review* article that these two feuding entities, whose work is deeply interconnected, each fail to value the other's contribution.

When marketing blames the sales force, the sales team, in turn, claims that marketing sets prices too high and uses too much of the budget. Sales teams also think that marketers are out of touch with what's going on with customers, while marketers think sales are too focused on the bottom line.

But when sales and marketing are fully integrated and focus on strategic, forward-thinking tasks both groups can share structures, systems, and rewards toward the same objective: the generation of profitable and increasing revenue. In fact, doing so makes all customer communications more integrated, as all teams are dedicated to promoting the same promise and USP. Profitability of the firm increases substantially - a result we call 'Force Multiplication'. This is due to either eliminating duplicate cost and / or reaping increased customer revenue and profits.

Managing Sales People: How to Make It Work

Many organizations take a 'big brother' and 'command and control' attitude towards their sales persons. Since sales people live or die via the empirical data of whether they met their quota, management has a tendency to burden sales people with the over-reporting of 'lost sales', sales pipelines, call reports, etc. Understandably, the management team wants visibility into the status of this month's or this quarter's revenue.

> *If companies are not careful, the relationship between management and sales people can break down to (a) distrust, (b) busy-work and (c) a pipeline of information that is full of junk. These are major reasons for the negative reviews of so many CRM implementations.*

CRM: Proceed with Caution

Customer Relationship Management (CRM) software had a rocky start when it was introduced in the 1980s. Within a decade it was adopted by Monster.com. The company spent more than a million dollars in an attempt to boost its sales force efficiency yet found the system to be inefficient and so slow that they had to rebuild the entire system. Technology has improved since then, and when CRM works, it provides methods for companies to:

- Gather information swiftly.

- Identify the most valuable customers over time.

- Control their customer data (e.g., the information resides centrally as opposed to decentralized in each sales person's files).

- Watch the workflow of their salespersons. The idea on workflow was that a company could compute each salespersons pipeline (e.g., 100 phone calls results in 10 presentations = one sale) into a predictive model of "closed sales."

If management noticed that the top-end of the sales funnel was low (e.g., too few phone calls were being made) to achieve the quota for "closed sales" they could counsel salespersons to make more phone calls. While the logic makes sense on one level, management failed to consider "what if" scenarios:

- What if CRM led sales persons to enter bogus information into the CRM system or perform busy-work to demonstrate that they were "trying hard?"

- What if it shifted the focus away from "closed sales?"

Previously, I demonstrated the concept of using a simple RFM (Recency, Frequency, and Monetary) value table to identify patterns in your company's customer data. Specifically, I highlighted the benefits of understanding your B-of-B customers – the likelihood that 10 percent of your customers generate 70+ percent of your revenue and profits.

Once you have established how many B-of-B and future "best" customers that transact with you recently (last three months) and frequently (12+ times per year), you can then establish B-of-B retention / growth goals and the acquisition of "best" prospects and Future B-of-B prospects.

This same logic in goal-setting directly applies to each salesperson. It's a short process:

1) Each salesperson should know the number of B-of-B and Future B-of-B that they do business with and establish retention and growth goals for each.

2) Each salesperson should establish B-of-B prospect and Future B-of-B prospect acquisition goals.

3) They should also establish a marketing calendar (next page) that includes the specific names of each in #1 and #2 above, and develop monthly marketing activities to each.

> *There is an alternative approach that satisfies the reporting needs of the corporate office, puts less burden on the salesperson with reporting busy work and keeps the salesperson empowered and focused on "closed sales."*

Example Marketing Budget and Calendar for Salespersons

Marketing Budget and Calendar July - September	12 Month Projected Value
Goals:	
Acquire 25 New Best of Best Customers @ $35,000 Each	$875,000
Acquire 25 New Future Best of Best Customers @ $8,000 Each	$200,000
Total Value	$1,075,000
Estimated Operating Margin	20%
Operating Margin Contribution	$215,000
Proposed Marketing Investment	$21,000
Estimated ROI	1024%

Action Plans	Responsible	July			August			September			Estimated Cost
BEST of BEST Customers											
Event 1 60 @ $50 / person	Sales/Mkt	X									$3,000
Event 2 60 @ $50 / person	Sales/Mkt							X			$3,000
Gift Shipment 50 @ $50 / person	Marketing				X						$2,500
Gift Shipment 50 @ $50 / person	Marketing		X								$2,500
Customer Lunch	Sales						X				$3,000
Future BEST of BEST Customers											
Gift Shipment 40 @ $50 / person	Marketing		X								$2,000
Gift Shipment 40 @ $50 / person	Marketing							X			$2,000
Testers	Sales										
Telemarketing welcome (outbound)		X	X	X	X	X	X	X	X	X	X	X	X	
Customer Experience – Create in-store experience (TV, soft drinks etc.)	Marketing		X								$3,000
											$21,000

This list should be provided to the marketing department so the marketing capital can be allocated and the marketing plan can be activated for each sales person. For a reporting basis, management simply needs to monitor the salespersons' goals vs. what has actually happened (e.g., goals vs. results).

This approach eliminates a tremendous amount of busy work - and keeps the eye on the prize: the number of closed deals. Each group (corporate, sales and marketing) are totally aligned towards achieving their common goal.

> *There is much more to marketing than product, pricing, place, and promotion, and there is much more to sales than pushing a commodity.*

Combining Forces

As companies become larger and more complex, some executives are now beginning to realize there is much more to marketing than product, pricing, place, and promotion, and there is much more to sales than pushing a commodity. By combining forces and tackling higher level tasks like segmenting their customers, there are widespread benefits for both the sales team and the marketing organization.

Through the techniques I've shared in prior chapters that focus on B-of-B customers, I have a remedy to align the marketing and sales organizations. Once the marketing and sales teams agree on the specific number of B-of-B customers and prospects to target, both organizations can work together on the tactics they employ.

As an example, if B-of-B customers and prospects have an annual revenue value to the organization of $35,000, and operating profit of $14,000, the sales and marketing teams might agree that $5,000 is an appropriate amount of marketing capital to allocate to retain and acquire each one.

Additionally, they can agree that a highly sought

> **By combining forces and tackling higher level tasks like segmenting their customers, there are widespread benefits for both the sales team and the marketing organization.**

after B-of-B customer or prospect sending a direct mail piece simply does not have the breakthrough force to capture the B-of-B customer's attention. Working together, the sales and marketing teams can engineer a marketing campaign targeted to each individual B-of-B customer or prospect that also leverages the strengths of each individual salesperson.

Marketing and sales can devise a simple campaign structure and then allow each individual salesperson to tailor the campaign to his/her own interests and their knowledge of the B-of-B. This is similar to the marketing calendar referenced in the last chapter that we use to get and retain customer loyalty. Here's an example of a conceptual campaign conducted four times a year:

- Mail a $100 gift with a personalized note from the salesperson. The purpose of this tactic is to use a gift to soften the beach-head, and open the customer or prospect to the idea of a face-to-face sales call.

- Hand-deliver a customized gift with a personalized note inviting the B-of-B to lunch with your CEO. The purpose of this action is to invoke a face-to-face sales call where the salesperson can demonstrate the value-add or competitive differentiators of his specific company. Hand-delivering the gift demonstrates sincere interest on behalf of the salesperson.

- After the face-to-face meeting with the B-of-B customer / prospect, the salesperson and your CEO, mail a follow-up note inviting the B-of-B and his or her spouse to a company sponsored philanthropic event that is important to your local community.

- After attending the event, send a thank-you note that acknowledges their attendance and shares with them the amount raised to support the charity. This is particularly effective if the customer has an affinity for a particular cause in which they donate time or money.

> *Marketing and sales can devise a simple campaign structure and then allow each individual salesperson to tailor the campaign to his/her own interests and their knowledge of the B-of-B.*

Once your marketing and sales teams have agreed upon a conceptual structure to the marketing campaign and the amount of capital to be invested, each individual salesperson can customize the campaign to suit their interests and their knowledge of each B-of-B customer or prospect.

In my position, I've done my homework and have solid information about our B-of-B customer base. On average, they have between 25 and 99 employees; 62 percent are in construction. What they really appreciate is dealing with local decision-makers like themselves.

We saw an opening in the market to be a premium service provider to this profile, and that's where we allocate our marketing budget. Currently, we spend over 80 percent of our marketing dollars on 10 percent of our base, and we do that to create the "right" kind of experience for them.

> *While one-to-one customization of a marketing campaign requires more effort, each salesperson is empowered with a specific amount of capital to tailor the marketing campaign within an agreed-upon framework. In other words, the salesperson is both empowered and accountable for the spending of marketing capital.*

Your company salesperson can tailor his or her own campaign in order to get in the door with a B-of-B customer, invoke empathy and develop a relationship.

Since marketing now involves the sales team in B-of-B customer / prospect selection, the recognition of the contribution value of the B-of-B, and the conceptual marketing tactics, the relationship between marketing (the cowboys) and sales (the sheriff and deputies) has shifted from adversarial to cooperative, from command and control, to highly decentralized.

This conceptual framework not only allows each sales person to flourish, but enables senior management and the marketing department to measure the results in a highly controlled manner and with

While one-to-one customization of a marketing campaign requires more effort, each salesperson is empowered with a specific amount of capital to tailor the marketing campaign within an agreed-upon framework.

Marketing
Supplies
Capital and
Tactics

Gift Basket
Event Hosting
Flowers
Gift Cards
Tickets

Sales
Chooses Tactics
From Menu
To Suit Client

capital allocated to the highest impact activities.

The end-result: a force multiplier.

Now that we know how to reach our "Best" customers through the combined forces of the sales and marketing teams, how do we reach the future "Best" and give them extra value? We next turn to how your company can acquire new B-of-B customers.

CONTRARIAN MARK**ᴲ**TING

CHAPTER FOURTEEN:
MARKETING STRATEGY AND FUTURE "BEST" CUSTOMERS WITH VALUE-ADDED SELLING

Chapter 14: Marketing Strategy and Future "Best" Customers with Value-Added Selling

> *"Thus those skilled in war subdue the enemy's army without battle. They conquer by strategy."*
>
> —Sun Tzu, The Art of War

The same process of outlining a marketing campaign to B-of-B customers can also be applied to the next tier of customers – or future B-of-B customers. While the first group represents a small percentage of the customer base and the largest portion of your revenue and profits, it's important to constantly groom *future* B-of-B customers that will transact more with your company. The idea here is that a company needs organic growth to maintain long-term profitability. Using historical terms from earlier in this book, the Rule of 80/20 is great for getting more from your B-of-B clientale, but increasing the popularity of your brand to the next tier of customers is often the best way to move more clients into the most profitable set.

For example, at Volvo Rents, our B-of-B represents 5 percent of the customer base and generates 73 percent of revenue. Each B-of-B customer spends $35,000 annually, generates $10,000 of operating profits, and transacts 24 or more times per year. Future B-of-B represents five percent of the customer base and generates 10 percent of revenue. These future B-of-B customers each spend about $8,000 annually, and generate operating profit of $3,000.

While one-to-one selling attention and $5,000 may be the appropriate amount of marketing capital to allocate to B-of-B customers and prospects, future B-of-B necessitate a different approach that makes them feel valued, without consuming as much selling time or marketing capital.

In working with the sales team, marketing can craft a $1,000 campaign that might include the following tactics:

- Quarterly gift or book mailing with a personalized note from the sales person. The mailing should include a customized report card about what your company did or did not do for the client. (For more pointers, read Tom Riley's book, *Value Added Selling,* in which Riley explains that if you provide a premium service or product, remind your customers of all that you do). For example: A $25,000 ad for Prada in the *NY Times* displays hand-stitched detail on their classic bags, sewn by craftsmen with more than 10 years experience in order to convey value for their super premium products; at Stew Leonard's $30+ million Connecticut grocery store, the store reminds customers why a nine dollar bottle of orange juice is a tremendous value and worth the price. Among the reasons: the oranges are hand-picked in optimal season, etc. Volvo Rents demonstrates the value of premium pricing by promoting its emergency services, spelling out its 24-hour service, no-questions-asked guarantee, and other customized benefits.

- Semi-annual invitations to a company-sponsored philanthropic event. Ask your future B-of-B customers and prospects to invite their co-workers to attend your event in supporting the local community.

- Semi-annual invitation to a company-sponsored event that is positioned as a 'learning opportunity'. Hire a recognized speaker or economist to give an update to your future B-of-B customers and prospects.

> *It's important that you constantly communicate 'value-add' to your customers and prospects, which subtly reminds them of all of the benefits that you offer them and why they should value you.*

With all of the marketing campaigns outlined above, it's important that you constantly communicate 'value-add' to your customers and prospects, which subtly reminds them of all of the benefits that you offer to them and why they should value *you*.

One owner of a retail store based in California says value-added selling is really a commitment to a particular *culture*, one that keeps the customer's perspective in mind while providing value without any additional cost.

"For example," he said, "we do quarterly reports for all of our customers that provide them and us with detailed information on the total amount of uptime in equipment rental, road call responses, and billing accuracy. Then we sit down and have an hour-long conversation with each customer to communicate that we want to make their experience better. There is no guess-work in this culture. We promise a high level of service but deliver more. Finally, we brag like heck about it to the customer – reinforcing what it is that we delivered."

Example 'Value-Addded' Selling Report.

Attn: The Boss
Your Best Customer
123 Build It Street
Construction, CA

	July-Sep 07	Aprl-Jun 07	Jan-Mar 07	Oct-Dec 06	12m Avg
Rental Equipment Up-time Report (% of total hours rental machines were up)	99.69%	99.68%	99.47%	99.59%	99.63%
On-Time Report (% of total deliveries made on-time)	100.00%	98.67%	99.11%	98.21%	98.95%
Road Call Response Time (hrs.) (avg. time from call to arrival on jobsite)	1.28	1.72	2.00	1.75	1.68
First Hour Break Downs (% total rentals with 1st hour breakdown)	0.00%	1.67%	0.00%	0.00%	0.40%
Billing Accuracy (% of total invoices billed correctly)	98.21%	98.28%	96.61%	96.61%	97.41%
On-Time Releases (hrs.) (avg. of time from request to return releases)	1.33	1.8	2.75	1.57	1.77

Value Added Services

26 July - ASAP Delivery Mini Excavator (Irvine) 1hr 30min
9 Aug - ASAP Delivery 2 Light Towers (Irvine) 1hr
16 Aug - ASAP Delivery Skid Steer (Perris) 55min
20 Aug - ASAP Delivery Mini Excavator (Riverside) 1hr 15min
23 Aug - ASAP Delivery Mini Excavator (Perris) 45min
7 Sep - ASAP Delivery 1-3 Ton Roller (Lake Elsinore) 40min
11 Sep - ASAP Delivery 1-3 Ton Roller (Temecula) 2hr 30min
11 SEP - Credit One Day Skip Loader (Missed Call Off)
11 SEP - Credit One Day Skip Loader (Missed Call Off)
11 SEP - Credit One Day Skip Loader (Missed Call Off)

"Every one of our customers knows that we provide this quarterly report," he said. "And every person that we've touched knows that we really care about them. The bottom line is that it's a matter of being proactive, not reactive."

He adds that if you don't find ways to clearly communicate that you are adding value to your customer, they will not fully appreciate why they do business with you. In one instance, late time was recorded as *less than a half percent* during a total of 196 deliveries – an impressive record that would have gone unnoticed by the customer had his staff not shared that information. Customers value on-time deliveries because they often have hundreds of workers, costing thousands of dollars, standing by to perform their work, all based on the equipment being delivered on time.

Here's a more detailed account of his month-by-month technique:

> *"We track on-time deliveries, equipment down-time and several other attributes so that we can demonstrate the value of excellent service to our customers. We don't mail this report to our customers. We personally visit our customers and/or decision makers to review each item. We ask if there is anything we can do to improve upon and add value to our relationship. This information and report saved a very good customer recently, due mainly to massive pressure on them to lower their prices. They got rental rates from five to seven other rental companies; some national brands as well as local and regional companies.*
>
> *We had to adjust some of our rates but in return we were guaranteed 100% of their business. Our business with this customer has dramatically increased so much that we added specific types of equipment in order to meet the demand. I cannot understate the effectiveness of this report. It takes a tremendous commitment to get this done but I believe it is worth it."*

This is a great example of a team that fully understands and applies the principles of value-added selling.

In Tom Riley's book *Value Added Selling* (McGraw Hill, 2003), he explains there are better ways to communicate with clients and implement a system of value-added techniques. Yet Riley said he felt like "a voice in the wilderness" when he first introduced his philosophy, a method that fit into five categories:

1. **The three dimensions** of value: the product, the company, and themselves.

2. **Dynamic blend**: a combination of both offensive and defensive selling initiatives. Offensive selling is pursuing new business. Defensive selling is protecting and growing existing business.

3. **Think strategically/sell tactically:** value-added sales people should both think and plan strategically before they execute their tactics.

4. **Proactive selling:** value-added sales people should add value, not cost. Rather than focus on how they can sell, they should concentrate on how to bring more value to the customer.

5. **A give and take relationship:** built on a win-win philosophy, it means contributing maximum value to the customer while extracting maximum value from the relationship.

Tom Riley's

5 categories of value-added selling

1. The three dimensions of value
2. Dynamic blend
3. Think strategically/sell tactically
4. Proactive selling
5. A give-and-take relationship

Source: Tom Riley's book Value Added Selling (McGraw Hill, 2003)

LIFETIME VALUE AS A CUSTOMER

Principles Underlying Contrarian Marketing:

- Customers comprise a corporate asset to be managed.

- Not all customers are created equal.

- If you optimize the Return on Investment (ROI) on customers, you optimize the value of the firm.

- Every marketing investment must PAY.

- Loyalty is the source of all profits.

Volvo Applies Value-Added Tactic

In one popular campaign strategy, a sales rep. had the local BBQ restaurant deliver lunches to a nearby job site since the workers were often too busy to stop and go elsewhere for a lunch break. The sales representative demonstrated the power of a personal touch. In exchange, the representative will get more value, more profit, and more loyalty from the customer.

Try This:

Now consider a real-life exercise related to your business. Define the experience that you want your B-of-B customers and future "Best" prospects to have.

This exercise should encompass every functional area within your company: Operations, Sales, Marketing, Finance, Information Technology and Human Resources. Each should be entirely focused on delivering a promise to your B-of-B customers.

Here's an outline to follow:

 Operations: communication of a "customer report card" or asking "What have we done for you lately?" This should include mistakes made and the resolution of problems.

 Sales: weekly contact with B-of-B customers. Portrayal of value-add, accessibility, flexibility, family involvement, access to senior management (e.g., your CEO and CFO) and the finest in professionalism.

 Marketing: value-add to the customer's business, flexibility, empathy, philanthropy and community involvement.

 Finance: accurate billing, flexibility in accounts receivable terms. Accounts receivable terms are your agreement with customers that establishes when the customer will pay you. Thirty days is standard for most businesses that extend payment terms.

Information Technology: systems that are accurate and easy to use, customer self-service applications (as needed).

Human Resources: flexibility with your employees. If you aim to build a cohesive culture, then treat your employees as B-of-B too. Involve your employees' families in your company events; involve your employees in the design of benefits programs; in how you treat them with sick time, time-off, etc. Each employee within your enterprise should know the list of B-of-B customers and prospects so that they can adjust their decision making to quickly and flexibly respond to the unique needs of your B-of-B customers and prospects. A happy employee is your best offense and defense in creating raving fans and protecting against your B-of-B going elsewhere, respectively.

Now that you know how adding value to your next best customers can increase loyalty and improve sales, doesn't it make sense to figure out a way to duplicate those efforts? You can, through cloning your B-of-B and future B-of-B customers.

> **The bottom line is you can run your business one of two ways:**
>
> (1) **Be a mass marketer and treat everyone equally and risk having your service or product become just a commodity or**
>
> (2) **Design a system and process to offer customized service to your customers in the way they want it—and in turn transform loyal customers into "raving fans".**

CONTRARIAN
MARK∃TING

CHAPTER FIFTEEN:
CLONING "BEST-OF-BEST" AND FUTURE "BEST" CUSTOMERS

Chapter 15: Cloning "Best-of-Best" and Future "Best" Customers

> *"Why not invest your assets in the companies you really like? As Mae West stated, 'Too much of a good thing can be wonderful.'"*
>
> **—Warren Buffet, investor**

In conventional marketing, there are many temptations from ad and online vendors to create prospects for your business.

Their value proposition is simple – they will help raise awareness for your business with the masses. While their claims may be true, their ability to create qualified leads of B-of-B and future B-of-B prospects is limited.

Do the math and consider whether your precious marketing capital is better served by staying focused on 'picking your customers, before they pick you'.

So how do you clone your B-of-B and future B-of-B customers? It involves both quantitative and qualitative methods which are easier than you think.

It's a simple, three-step process with help available through resources provided at the end of the book.

Basically, here's what you do:

1. Export a list of your B-of-B and future B-of-B customers (those who transact 24+ times with your business). Note: you will want to customize the selection criteria to your business.

2. Send this list to a database research company and ask the research company to append attributes on the database. Cost is minimal relative to the information you will receive.

   a. Market research firms use publicly available databases (Experian, Dun & Bradstreet, and InfoUsa) to access information about your customers. Rest assured, this is an entirely 'legal' process, and your customers have agreed to products / services that they use.

b. The data append process should involve criteria like SIC codes (standard industrial codes), company revenue, number of employees, location, credit rating and key contact information.

c. Have the Market Research company run a pattern analysis to tell you the percentage of customers you have based on the attributes identified above.

3. Draw your conclusions:

    a. With which customers are you most popular?

        i. Small companies

        ii. Big Companies

        iii. Industries

        iv. Those you can measure by revenue.

        v. Those you can measure by number of employees.

        vi. Companies with certain types of credit scores.

        vii. Companies with single locations or multiple locations .

        viii. Those in which you generally deal with the owner; project manager; or a line employee.

Qualitatively, the process is equally as simple. Involve your sales people, marketing team, operations people and other employees, and discuss the conclusions that they draw from the analysis. What conclusions did you reach?

Using specific questions may help:

1. Why do companies of certain sizes do business with you?

    a. Flexibility

    b. Relationship

    c. Convenience

    d. What else?

> So how do you clone your B-of-B and future B-of-B customers? It involves both quantitative and qualitative methods which are easier than you think. It's a simple, three-step process with help available through resources provided at the end of the book.

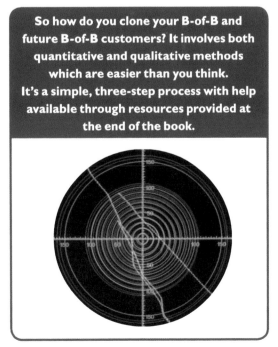

2. Why do various industries do business with you?

    a. Flexibility

    b. Relationship

    c. Convenience

    d. What else?

3. What about companies that have variable credit scores? In performing this analysis, keep in mind that companies usually only want to do business with those who have a solid record of paying their bills on time.

4. Are the business locations single or multiple?

5. Are you dealing with the owner or other employees?

6. Why do they value you? For example:

    a. Because of the relationship they have with you.

    b. Because of great service.

7. Are they price-sensitive? Or do they appreciate the value that you offer to them?

8. Are they willing to pay a price premium?

While simple, the purpose of this process is to identify patterns and determine a framework of why the B-of-B customers and future B-of-B customers do business with you.

Cloning B-of-B and Future B-of-B

To clone these two types of customers, the process is equally as simple:

1. Access publicly available prospect databases such as InfoUSA, Experian or Dun and Bradstreet, to name a few.

2. Input the key criteria based on the conclusions from your data matching process:

    a. Industry

    b. Company size – by revenue.

    c. Company size – by number of employees.

d. Location – proximity to your business.

e. Publicly owned or entrepreneur owned business.

3. Download the list based on the appropriate radius around your business. (e.g., 5, 10, or 25 miles, etc.).

What conclusions do you reach when reviewing the list? A few more questions:

• Do you recognize the companies on the list?

• Which of your competitors are they doing business with? Why?

• Do they have a good reputation?

• Would they value the type of product and service that your company offers?

If you are unfamiliar with some of the companies, have your sales persons visit the sites and determine the fit with your company.

While all of these will require an investment of time, the more time and effort you put into research, the more likely you are to achieve the results that you want: picking your B-of-B and future B-of-B customers before they pick you.

I believe so strongly in the power of data that I already feel we can pick our customers before they pick us. We structure our local marketing plans around events rather than postcard mailings or magazine ads. And we stick to this game plan, positioning the local decision-maker in each market as the "hero," which translates to more cookouts, more free gourmet coffee in our customer's hands, more ensuring that our operations know who their best customers are - from the manager, to the driver, to the yard worker. We also host regional customer events, from hunting and fishing trips to NASCAR races.

> **_The more time and effort you put into research, the more likely you are to achieve the results that you want._**

This strategy gives equal weight to nurturing existing B-of-B customers and mining for new customers that fit the B-of-B profile. I visited one of our owners at a multi-store operation with 5,000 customers. I found that 171 (less than five percent of customers) generate about 70 percent of the revenues and the majority of profits. We, of course, want to make sure we're really marketing to those folks in order to make them feel valued.

But what about the other 107 future B-of-B people on the list? Can we make them feel special too? Can we engender loyalty and ultimately earn more of their business?

While we know that only a small portion of customers do a large percentage of business, those few at the top (the B-of-B) transact more than 10 times a year. Each of the top tier customer's value individualized services catering to their unique needs. Any business should be happy to provide individual services because they profit greatly from those few customers.

Breaking It Down: What One Smart Hospital Did

El Camino Hospital in Mountain View, California, figured out that carefully selecting their customers helped to generate revenue and control costs.

Specifically, they looked at the aggregated experience of their cardiology base. The focus was on acquisition and volume, but the approach was on maximizing relationships with existing patients. They identified the type of services patients used outside cardiology and found out what each patient spent on individual transactions, such as visits to the emergency department.

This strategy provided them with a road map in areas that had a high concentration of desired targets, including the over-55 population that could benefit from vascular disease screenings. More than 8,000 households received an invitation to register for a free screening and the mailing list was entered in the hospital's database. By deleting households that were already El Camino patients, the campaign culled brand new "potential patients."

El Camino Hospital in Mountain View, California, figured out that carefully selecting their customers helped to generate revenue and control costs.

Within three days of the mailings receipt, available slots were filled and there was a waiting list of 250 people. (The goal was 216 from the 8,000 mailings.) As an added bonus, the hospital culled goodwill from the project.

In the next chapter you'll find a description of some of the tools you'll need to find, keep, and maintain those B-of-B customers.

CONTRARIAN
MARK**E**TING

BUILDING THE CUSTOMER MODEL WITH A
BUDGETED MARKETING PLAN

Chapter 16: Building the Customer Model with a Budgeted Marketing Plan

> *"Breakthrough ideas are around the corner*
>
> *but most of us are failing to take a chance on them."*
>
> —Larry Page, Google founder

As a reader, and hopefully as a convert to **Contrarian Marketing**, you have made tremendous progress. We've discussed the importance of B-of-B customers and prospects to your business, and how to construct a de-centralized model whereby sales persons have the liberty to customize the execution of the marketing plan to their individual customers.

Most of you are familiar with a marketing plan: a document that displays your recommendations for a business and its sales team. It describes your goals, strategies, tactics and objectives and exactly how you plan to achieve them. There are two main reasons people write marketing plans: to communicate the plan and to gain support for it.

Contrarian Marketing will show you an easy five-minute way to achieve all of that. The concept of the customer model is a simple Microsoft Excel spreadsheet, whereby a salesperson can map out his or her marketing strategy to earn more business from B-of-B customers and acquire more B-of-B prospects.

At the top of the customer model simple calculations help identify the number of B-of-B customers / prospects and future B-of-B prospects that each salesperson is seeking.

Their goals should mirror your corporate data. For instance, if 10 percent of your customers generate 70+ percent of revenue and profit, that is what each sales person should seek. In addition, they should strive to add B-of-B prospects and future B-of-B prospects at an equivalent level.

As an example:

Step 1: Quantify your existing B-of-B and Future B-of-B customers and their annual spending with your company.

EXISTING CUSTOMERS

25 B-of-B customers spending $35,000 each, annually

25 Future B-of-B customers spending $8,000 each, annually

Step 2: Establish your goals in the number of prospective B-of-B and Future B-of-B customers that you aim to acquire and their annual spending targets.

PROSPECTS

25 B-of-B prospects spending $35,000 each, annually

25 Future B-of-B prospects spending $8,000 each, annually

The retention of just 50 B-of-B customers, and the acquisition of 50 B-of-B prospects and future B-of-B prospects will double the sales persons revenue and their contributions to your profits.

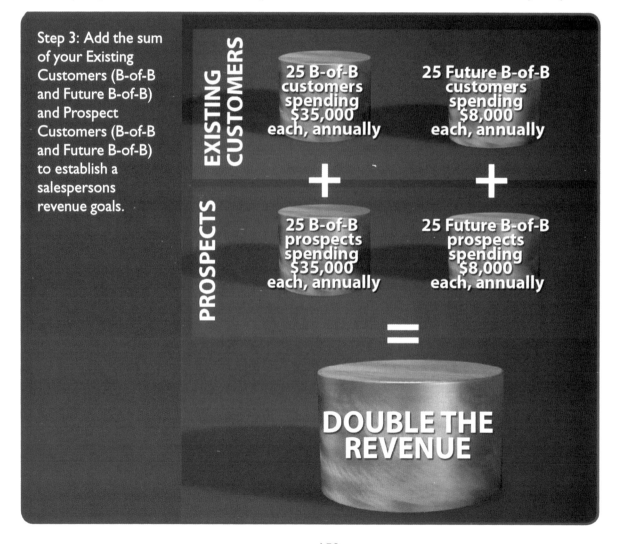

Step 3: Add the sum of your Existing Customers (B-of-B and Future B-of-B) and Prospect Customers (B-of-B and Future B-of-B) to establish a salespersons revenue goals.

EXISTING CUSTOMERS

25 B-of-B customers spending $35,000 each, annually

25 Future B-of-B customers spending $8,000 each, annually

+   +

PROSPECTS

25 B-of-B prospects spending $35,000 each, annually

25 Future B-of-B prospects spending $8,000 each, annually

=

DOUBLE THE REVENUE

Let's keep going.

In the left hand column (the X axis), the sales person should list their B-of-B customers and prospects. Across the top row (the Y axis), the salesperson should list the months of the year.

Starting with the first B-of-B customer, and working their way down to B-of-B prospects, the salesperson should write into each month the marketing activity.

> *Typical marketing activities should revolve around relationship marketing techniques that include value-added selling: communicating to the customer how your company will deliver the promises made, and how it will meet the customer's expectations.*

Here's what you want your B-of-B customers to value most about your company:

- Flexibility
- Responsiveness
- Prestige
- Cost-savings

- Affiliation
- Transformational technology
- Business acumen / precision
- Frequency of contact

For each customer, from left-to-right, have each sales person type in the marketing tactic for the customer by month and add a dollar amount. The strategic direction for the marketing tactic should be derived from the corporate marketing department on the most effective marketing tactics.

For instance, in January invite the client to a charity fund-raiser at a cost to the company of $500; send the client a $100 gift in February; bring lunch to the client and staff in March at a cost of $75, etc.

Be sure the marketing tactic concept is consistent with the agreement between the marketing and sales team, and represents your company's value proposition.

In the example "Marketing Budget and Marketing Calendar" on the next page, goals and activities are outlined over a six-month period. The marketing department and sales team are responsible for the items noted.

In this example "Marketing Budget and Marketing Calendar", goals and activities are outlined over a six-month period.

Marketing Budget and Calendar July - September	12 Month Projected Value
Goals:	
Acquire 100 New Best of Best Customers @ $35,000 Each	$3,500,000
Acquire 200 New Future Best of Best Customers @ $8,000 Each	$1,600,000
Total Value	$5,100,000
Estimated Operating Margin	20%
Operating Margin Contribution	$1,020,000
Proposed Marketing Investment	$45,000
Estimated ROI	2,263%

For a larger view of the "Marketing Budget and Marketing Calendar", refer to page 175 in the Appendix.

Week		JUN	JUL	AUG	SEP	OCT	NOV	DEC	COSTS
Pull prospect list based on research and cloning of 'Best of the Best' Customers	Marketing Department								
Research of Prospect List the very best of prospects. Goal is to 'Pick Your Customers' before they pick you- prioritize the list of top 100 / 200 prospects that have the potential to transact 24+ and 12+ / Year.	Salesperson	X							
Best of the Best' customers and prospects									
Frequency: 12-23 and 24+ per year									
Customer Events - Invite Created (2 mailings - Invite and Save the Date)	Marketing Dept.		X		X				$480
Event 1- $5,000. Target cost per person = $50. Target 100 attendees.	Salesperson & Marketing Dept.			X		X			$5,000
Event 2- $5,000. Target cost per person = $50. Target 100 attendees.	Salesperson & Marketing Dept.								$5,000
Customer Lunches - 2X / month ($12/person x 25 person avg)	Salesperson		X	X	X	X	X	X	$3,600
Gift shipment 1 with note (order placed) ($50 / each) - 100 customers.	Marketing Dept.		X						$5,000
Gift shipment 2 with note (order placed) ($50 / each). 100 customers.	Marketing Dept.		X						$5,000
Gift 3: 1:1 Visits with Top Customers (1x / week) * 2 sales people (Top Down Selling) with hand-delivered gifts ($10 / each). 200 ccustomers	Salesperson				X				$2,000
Future Best Customers & Prospects: Goal is to acquire 200 new 'future best of the best customers' who transact 6-11 times per year.									
-6x to 11x /Year									
Monitor 80/20 CRM Data	Salesperson	X	X	X	X	X	X		
Gift Shipment 1 w/ personalized note. 200 prospects x $10 each.	Owner / Marketing Dept		X						$2,000
Gift Shipment 2 w/ personalized note. 200 prospects x $10 each.	Owner / Marketing Dept								$2,000
Gift Shipment 3 w/ personalized note. 200 prospects x $10 each.	Owner / Salesperesons					X			$2,000
Gift Shipment 4 w/ personalized note. 200 prospects x $10 each.	Owner / Salesperesons						X		$2,000
Testers									
-1x - 5x / Year									
Monitor 80/20 CRM Data	Junior Salesperson	X	X	X	X	X	X		
Use outbound tele-marketing to welcome new customers to your business	Junior Salesperson		X	X	X	X	X		
Customer Experience									
Create the 'customer experience' by building an in-store 'experience' area. As an example, the Volvo Rents Contractors Corner: robust sound system inside and /outside, Pepsi soda fountain, Refridgerator w/ favorite foods & energy drinks, big screen TV, comfortable couches, sports memorabilia, photos off employees & customers families, etc.)	Owner / Salespersons / Delivery / Wak-In		X						$5,000
Referral Vouchers - $100 each (redemption @ 20%). Designed to invoke trial - give customers a reason to visit the store. Target 10 referrals / month.	Marketing Dept / Marketing	X	X	X	X	X	X	X	$6,000
									$45,080

The goals are to create $5,100,000 in value creation from new B-of-B customers and future B-of-B customers:

Example: Acquire 100 new B-of-B Customers @ $35,000 each = $3,500,000 in value creation.

Example: Acquire 200 new Future B-of-B Customers @ $8,000 each = $1,600,000 in value creation.

With an estimated 20 percent operating margin for B-of-B and future B-of-B customers, net gain in operating margin equals $1,020,000.

The marketing campaign, executed with a coordinated effort between the marketing and sales teams, requires an investment of $45,000. The projected ROI (return on investment) is estimated to be 2,263%.

CUSTOMER MODEL

REVENUE GOAL	$	5,100,000					
ESTIMATED OPERATING MARGIN	$	20%					
OPERATING MARGIN CONTRIBUTION	$	1,020,000					

CUSTOMER	#	S/CUSTOMER/YEAR	EXTENDED	% to TTL Rev.	GROSS MARGIN %	GM DOLLARS	% to TTL MARGIN
BEST OF BEST	100	$ 35,000	$ 3,500,000	69%	25%	$ 860,650	84%
FUTURE BEST OF BEST	200	$ 8,000	$ 1,800,000	31%	10%	$ 160,000	16%
TOTAL	200		$ 5,100,000	100%		$ 1,020,650	100%

AVG. S / CUSTOMER
$ 17,000

The following graphic represents a customer model (how many customers are needed; how much revenue/profit they will create). This enables the marketing and sales team to operate from the same sheet of music.

By defining your customer and prospect targets, and defining the marketing activities to breakthrough to each of the customer segmentations, you can harness your company's efforts into a highly effective marketing campaign.

> *While the corporate office can and should establish the marketing strategy and framework, it is essential that you involve each field office and employee in establishing a budget that each field office & salesperson considers their own for use in their local market.*

Begin by using a percentage of projected revenue and profits for the field office and salesperson. One to eight percent is generally a reasonable allocation for marketing.

The corporate marketing organization should then establish the allocation of marketing capital and have a framework of tactics that each field office / sales person can choose from.

As an example, assuming that all marketing tactics have equal marketing effects:

Relationship marketing (Events, etc):	20 percent
Surprise & Delight Gifts:	20 percent
Philanthropic Marketing:	20 percent
Customer Experience: *In-store signage, sound systems, fragrance systems*	20 percent
Internet marketing; printed collateral	20 percent

With individual budgets, field offices and salesperson are now empowered to activate their own marketing campaigns to their B-of-B customers and B-of-B prospects using the corporate marketing organization for the execution of the campaign.

The field simply gives direction on which bucket they are accessing, provides the list of B-of-B customers / prospects they are targeting and provide direction on the type of personalization they require.

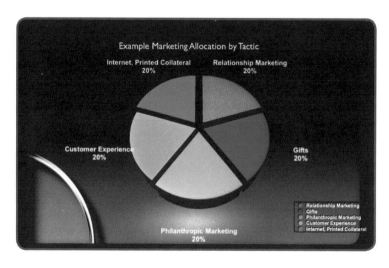

> *Based on the direction from the field office and salespersons, the corporate marketing organization can "localize" and "personalize" every marketing campaign by customer type. This is just as the local salesperson should be able to pick and choose from the available marketing tactics to customize the campaign to each of his/her customers.*

A salesperson in the Midwest devised a list of 20 major prospective B-of-B customers with whom he could not establish a connection. If he could acquire these prospects, he determined that he could double his business within one year, as he estimated that each customer had an annual value of $50,000. To activate the campaign, he:

- Sent the list of 20 prospective B-of-B customers to the corporate marketing department.

- Requested that they devise a "surprise & delight" gift campaign with a target spend of $50 each. Since the prospects were major national companies, he requested the gift consist of food items that were thoughtful, but would not be considered "over-the top."

The gift, consisting of food items sourced from gourmet purveyors in the region, was sent along with a personalized note from the sales person introducing his company and himself.

The results: five prospects immediately responded, each with the potential to spend up to $50,000, and each requested a scheduled appointment.

In the end, five of the Future B-of-B prospects became customers with a projected annual spend rate of $50,000 each, and the marketing campaign generated a substantial return on investment (ROI).

> *In the end, five of the Future B-of-B prospects became customers with a projected annual spend rate of $50,000 each.*

How Much Marketing is Too Much Marketing?

We all have limits of course on how much data we can absorb. What about marketing? How much is too much?

Some consulting firms say marketers have a tendency to launch too many messages across multiple channels and hope that something will stick.

It's important, they explain, to have a clear idea of your objectives before you can define your target segment and attempt to tailor your message. Marketing solution vendors know this, and offer a variety of products and services to help businesses store and analyze their marketing and campaign data.

But when do you reach a saturation point with *too much marketing?* Since customers receive literally thousands of advertising messages daily, there is a real danger you will be tuned out despite your best efforts. Or, as one marketing researcher stated, "What happens when your five percent relevant message becomes 95 percent noise?"

> *One of your best defenses is to have a clear idea of your objectives before you engage in any major marketing effort.*

In other words, define your market segment, determine what they value, tailor your message to meet that targeted market, and develop an integrated marketing communications plan to present this message to customers.

"Anything that isn't working is too much," stated Joseph Manos, executive V.P. of MindFireInc, which provides direct mail tracking software. He says customers are more turned off by irrelevant messages that repeat. But he says there is no such thing as "too much" when the message itself has real value (*Customer Relationship Management*, Oct. 2008).

In the final chapter we'll provide a few tactics you can apply to **Contrarian Marketing** methods along with a recap of the major points discussed throughout the text.

CONTRARIAN
MARK∃TING

CONTRARIAN MARKETING TACTICS-A RECAP

Chapter 17: Contrarian Marketing Tactics–A Recap

> *"We don't have to be smarter than the rest; we have to be more*
>
> *disciplined than the rest."*
>
> —*Warren Buffet, investor*

In business-to-business and business-to-consumer marketing, there are countless options for marketing tactics: search engine marketing, direct mail, special events, email marketing, newsletters, radio, TV, newspapers, magazines, promotional products, and customer loyalty programs.

One of the newer and least understood strategies is Integrated Marketing Communications (IMC), a coordinated marketing communications process which focuses on uniting a company's communication efforts across disciplines in order to magnify the delivery of the USP.

When pursuing any marketing tactic, you should consider how your competition is marketing to your B-of-B customers and your prospective B-of-B.

Then ask:
- What tactics or delivery vehicles are they using?
- How much are they spending per impression?
- What message are they trying to deliver?
- What price, service, or innovation are they providing?
- Are they engaging in flexibility and relationship-building?
- Are they using the same tactic on all of their customers, or are they tailoring the tactic based upon the potential value of the customer or prospect to their business?
- Are they tailoring the tactic to the influencers that surround the decision-maker?

In addition, find out who is competing for your prospect's attention by asking what tactics or delivery vehicles they use and how much they are spending per impression.

As an example, if you are targeting a C-level executive, that person probably receives an incredible volume of e-mails, letters, direct mail pieces, magazine subscriptions and promotional products (e.g., notepads, pens, mugs, hats, etc.) - with little, if any time, to review each.

Chances are, all of the above end up in the trash. If a business spent $10 to $20 to launch a campaign to a C-level prospect, can you think of a better way to send that $10 or $20 so that it breaks through to the prospect by separating itself from everything else that person receives on a daily basis?

The point is to take time to find out your customers' or prospects' personality and lifestyle. What do they like to do? Tailor the item based on your hypothesis about what you think matches their personality and lifestyle.

In Summary:

Always question what marketing tactic is likely to break through and be remembered. Are you sending 20 direct mail pieces for $1 each or one gift mailing for $20?

Always aim to use different marketing tactics as opposed to what your competitors are doing. *Be contrarian.*

> ***Always aim to use different marketing tactics as opposed to what your competitors are doing. Be contrarian.***

Always ask yourself what emotion or call-to-action you want to elicit:

- Do you want an appointment?
- Are you trying to build a relationship?
- Are you trying to sell something immediately?

Always personalize the messaging to your B-of-B customers and your B-of-B prospects.

Once you have identified the tactics that you want to use, schedule the series of tactics to each B- of-B customer and prospect, so that they hear from you on a frequent basis. After you've established the frequency and the tactics, you can quickly sum the dollar value of marketing to each. You now can calculate the cost per qualified lead for your marketing campaign.

Contrarian Marketing **Recap:**

A common trap in customer service is the old expression—"If I make an exception for you, Mr. Customer, I have to make an exception for everyone."

But what if 'Mr. Customer' is not everybody? What if he or she is a B-of-B, the 10 percent segment that creates 80 percent of your revenue and profits?

What if the B-of-B customer spends 20 times more than your average customer? Get a grip and change the rules for B-of-B customers. It's up to you to design the processes, business systems, technology, tools, or human intelligence to identify and hang onto the B-of-B customers at all cost.

By contrast, have you ever noticed the customers that complain the most are often the low-value customers to your organization? They are typically the scammers, the ones looking for the 'gotcha' or any excuse to get a freebie.

Now, think about your B-of-B customers. They rarely complain, follow the rules, say thank you—if anything, they shun personal attention and special favors. However, be careful…offend them once, make them feel like a number, treat them with disrespect, and you'll never see them again. They can get your product or service from your competitor.

contrarian marketing

What if the B-of-B customer spends **20 times** **more than your average customer?**

The five most important points from *Contrarian Marketing*:

1 Consciously plan and execute the B-of-B system that I have outlined in this book. Design simple, easy-to-use systems for B-of-Bs that are fail-safe in ensuring that your top customers receive B-of-B service and recognition. Give employees a simple mechanism in which they can stay aware of their B-of-B customers, and then grant them the authority to make decisions in order to accommodate those customers.

2 Attention Management: design your system to track what you are doing for B-of-B customers. If you are tracking metrics, why aren't there more exceptions for B-of- B customers?

3 Learn from every experience why an employee made a decision to ignore or miscast a "Best of the Best." Mistakes on your employees' part are fine. But limiting repetition of mistakes is the key. Validate through your management systems that the B-of-B recipient is indeed a B-of-B customer.

4 If all else fails, apologize quickly to your B of B customers. Lavish them with a special gift. Before you know it, you may just turn your organization's gaffe into yet an even better B-of-B customer.

5 Most important, "Protect and Serve" your best customers, even if means turning contrarian in your approach. Dare to swim upstream.

It all comes down to designing customized service within your VIP customer base. You have to make choices in business that you cannot be all things to all people. This is especially true in our current economic climate. As of early 2011, consumer confidence continued to remain shaky with the ominous specter of higher unemployment, more Washington gridlock and possibly even inflation ahead.

> *It all comes down to designing customized service within your VIP customer base. You have to make choices in business that you cannot be all things to all people. This is especially true in our current economic climate.*

Put simply: when your best customers ask for something out of the ordinary, say yes. If they want to call you at home, say yes. If they want a midnight delivery, say yes.

Make their long term value so important to your organization that when they do call, they get your undivided attention. Treat them differently from the herd; make them special. If you do, you will have a customer for life.

My premise in **Contrarian Marketing** is straightforward; the message clear. Or as any 'winning' Blackjack player will tell you, "It's not magic, just math."

CONTRARIAN
MARK3TING

MARKETING RESOURCES

Our customized resources include:

1) **Facilitated Contrarian Marketing Training:** We offer facilitated training for the core concepts in **Contrarian Marketing** customized to your business. Contact us to see how we can help leverage these power principles in **Contrarian Marketing** into your sales workforce. Visit **www.contrarianmarketingseminars.com** for more information.

2) **Workshops:** In addition, we offer facilitated workshops to apply the core concepts in **Contrarian Marketing** customized to your business. Our workshops allow you to bring your data with you to discover your Best of Best (B-of-B) customers and go home with results. Contact us to see how we can help leverage these power principles in **Contrarian Marketing.**

3) **Keynote Presentation:** Need a message to drive home the power of **Contrarian Marketing?** Let us help channel your company's energies with a keynote presentation and training to refocus your team's marketing and sales efforts.

4) **Bi-Weekly Dashboards:** Every two weeks, you will receive a dashboard highlighting changes in your customer base over the past year. The dashboards have been enhanced to show changes in your customer base. They include recommended actions based on these trends:

   • Recency/Frequency/Monetary (RFM) Value data
   • Product purchased or rented in the current year
   • A complete list of your customers and changes by segment

5) **Quarterly Market Dashboards:** Quarterly, you will receive a dashboard showing market projections for your Metropolitan Statistical Areas (MSA). The dashboards will show projections for the value of econometric data for your area, overall GDP, employment, and total employment by numerous categories; econometric data elements that are most important in your markets. Additionally, you will also receive GDP data for multiple categories as we define with you.

6) **Metropolitan Statistical Area (MSA) Maps:** Upon request, receive a map for your respective MSAs showing expected econometric activity in 2013 & 2015, competitors, and population change by ZIP code.

7) **Population and Econometric Dynamics by MSA:** If interested, you can order a population and econometric dynamics report by MSA. These 30- to 50-page reports are

packed with information about your local market. They include detailed data on long-term population changes, earnings and cost-of-living, number of changes, earnings and cost-of-living, number of competing companies and the estimated center of econometric activity.

8) **Customer Transaction Data:** Get information on the amount and type of transactions by companies in your area where, for example, a Universal Commercial Code (UCC) filing has been made. You may use this to enhance your prospect list. Some of the data are free,while other data can be purchased based upon your needs.

(Customer Classification: We have firmographic data for many of your customers.) The data includes Standard Industry Code (SIC)/NAICS industry class, number of employees, subsidiary or stand-alone, etc. You can use this data to look for similar companies in your prospect base. Combining this with ZIP code data on customers in your area, you can also evaluate the percentage of customers you have versus those in the market. Additionally, we can run a custom analysis of your customer base on contact names that can be used to estimate gender and ethnicity. There is a fee for producing this type of data as we purchase this data from third parties.

9) **Custom Analysis:** By providing us with your transaction data, we can develop custom reports for you to answer questions; as in what makes your best customers 'best' (frequency of usage, amount spent on each transaction, value of what's spent, etc.); how customers have migrated over time; any cross-sell opportunities, etc.

In addition, there are a number of marketing research resources available through the *Contrarian Marketing* website at **www.contrarianmarketingseminars.com**.

CONTRARIAN
MARK**3**TING

WORKS CITED

Introduction

www.aspousa.org

Wall Street Journal, 11/08/04

Wall Street Journal, 08/05/10

Advertising Age, 12/08/08

Advertising Age, 02/14/05

The 80/20 Principle, by R. Koch, 1998

Bringing Down the House: Inside Story of Six M.I.T. Students Who Took Vegas for Millions, by B. Mezrich, 2008 (Reprint)

The Virtual Corporation, Davidow & Malone

Chapter One

Bringing Down the House, pg 83

Stanford Graduate School of Business, Case GS-50, 10/07/03

Angel Customers & Demon Customers, by L. Selden, Portfolio Hardcover 2003

Wall Street Journal, 12/16/09

Wall Street Journal, 07/30/10

USA Today, 03/11/10

Incentive #180. 2006

Fortune, 03/16/09

Fortune #6, 2006

Sales & Marketing, #158, 2006

http://gaming.univer.edu

Chapter Two

Time, 02/02/10

Wall Street Journal, 04/02/08

CNBC.com by A. Crippen, 06/22/09

Chapter Three

Inc, Oct 2009

www.PCWorld.com, Consumer Watch, Oct 2007

Chapter Four

www.marketo.com/dg2-lead-nurturing

Sales & Marketing Management, March 2005

Chapter Five

None

Chapter Six

1984, by George Orwell

Moneyball: The Art of Winning an Unfair Game, by M. Lewis, 2003

Wall Street Journal, 04/02/07

ABA Bank Marketing, Oct 2006

Advertising Age, 2009

Chapter Seven

Deliver Magazine, 12/07

Marketing Tools, May 1996 Vol 3

University of VA Darden School Foundation 2005

Chapter Eight

www.hertz.com

Chapter Nine

The Art of War, Sun Tzu

CIO Decisions, June 2005

Chapter Ten

The Experience Economy, by J. Pines & J. Gilmore, 1998

Business Week, 07/13/10

Forbes, 07/24/09

Business Horizons, 2005

Hospitality Design, July 2010

Chapter Eleven

Forbes 10/30/09

Way of the Shepherd: Seven Ancient Secrets to Many Productive People, K. Leman & W. Pentak, 2010

Volvo Way Brand Management presentation

Chapter Twelve

Business Week, 07/13/10

Chapter Thirteen

Harvard Business Review, July-August 2006

Chapter Fourteen

Value-Added Selling, T. Riley 2003

Chapter Fifteen

Healthcare Financial Management, July 2005

Chapter Sixteen

None

Chapter Seventeen

Customer Relationship Management, October 2008

Look for updates on our website at *www.contrarianmarketingseminars.com.*

CONTRARIAN
MARK=TING

RECOMMENDED READING

Art of War, Sun Tzu, iUniverse, 2002

Brand Sense, by Martin Lindstrom, Free Press, 2005

Bringing Down the House, by Ben Mezrich, Free Press, 2008

Angel Customers and Demon Customers, by Larry Selden, Portfolio Hardcover, 2003

80/20 Principle, by Richard Koch, Doubleday, 1998; 2008

The Experience Economy, by B. Joseph Pine and James H. Gilmore Harvard Business Press, 1999

Flawless Execution, by James D. Murphy, Harper Collins, 2005

How to Win Friends & Influence People, by D. Carnegie, Pocket Books, 1990

The Ice Cream Maker, by Subir Chowdhury, Doubleday Currency, 2005

Managing Brand Equity, David A. Aacker, Free Press,

Marketing 3.0, by Philip Kotler. 2010

Moneyball, by Michael Lewis, 2003

Raving Fans, by Ken Blanchard, William Morrow, 1993

Sam Walton: Made in America, Bantam, 1993

Thinking for a Living, by Thomas H. Davenport, Harvard Business School Press, 2005

Value-Added Selling, by Tom Reilly, McGraw-Hill, 2002

The Warren Buffett Way, 2nd Edition, by R. Hagstrom, Jr., 1997

The Way of the Shepherd, by Dr. Kevin Leman and William Pentak, Zondervan, 2010

Word of Mouth Marketing, by A. Senovitz, Kaplan Publishing, 2006; 2009

Look for updates on our website at *www.contrarianmarketingseminars.com.*

CONTRARIAN
MARK**E**TING

APPENDIX

Example Marketing Calendar

Week		JUN	JUL	AUG	SEP	OCT	NOV	DEC	COSTS
Pull prospect list based on research and cloning of 'Best of the Best' Customers	Marketing Department								
Research of Prospect List the very best of prospects. Goal is to Pick Your Customers' before they pick you- prioritize the list of top 100 / 200 prospects that have the potential to transact 24+ and 12+ / Year.	Salesperson	X							
Best of the Best' customers and prospects									
Frequency: 12-23 and 24+ per year									
Customer Events - Invite Created (2 mailings- Invite and Save the Date)	Marketing Dept.		X		X				$480
Event 1: $5,000. Target cost per person = $50. Target 100 attendees.	Salesperson & Marketing Dept.			X		X			$5,000
Event 2: $5,000. Target cost per person = $50. Target 100 attendees.	Salesperson & Marketing Dept.		X		X				$5,000
Customer Lunches - 2X / month ($12/person x 25 person avg)	Salesperson		X	X	X	X	X	X	$3,600
Gift shipment 1 with note (order placed) ($50 / each) - 100 customers.	Marketing Dept.		X						$5,000
Gift shipment 2 with note (order placed) ($50 / each). 100 customers	Marketing Dept		X						$5,000
Gift 3: 1:1 Visits with Top Customers (1x / week) * 2 sales people (Top Down Selling) with hand-delivered gifts ($10 / each). 200 ccustomers	Salesperson			X					$2,000
Future Best Customers & Prospects: Goal is to acquire 200 new 'future best of the best customers' who transact 6-11 times per year.									
-6x to 1x / Year									
Monitor 80/20 CRM Data	Salesperson	X	X	X	X	X	X		
Gift Shipment 1 w/ personalized note. 200 prospects x $10 each.	Owner / Marketing Dept		X		X		X		$2,000
Gift Shipment 2 w/ personalized note. 200 prospects x $10 each.	Owner / Marketing Dept		X	X					$2,000
Gift Shipment 3 w/ personalized note. 200 prospects x $10 each.	Owner / Salespersons				X				$2,000
Gift Shipment 4 w/ personalized note. 200 prospects x $10 each.	Owner / Salespersons					X			$2,000
Testers									
-1x - 5x / Year									
Monitor 80/20 CRM Data	Junior Salesperson		X	X	X	X	X		
Use outbound tele-marketing to welcome new customers to your business	Junior Salesperson		X	X	X	X	X		
Customer Experience									
Create the 'customer experience' by building an in-store 'experience' area. As an example, the Volvo Rents Contractors Corner: robust sound system inside and /outside, Pepsi soda fountain, Refridgerator w/ favorite foods & energy drinks, big screen TV, comfortable couches, sports memorabilia, photos off employees & customers families, etc.)	Owner / Salespersons / Delivery / Walk-In		X						$5,000
Referral Vouchers - $100 each (redemption @ 20%). Designed to invoke trial - give customers a reason to visit the store. Target 10 referrals / month.	Marketing Dept / Marketing	X	X	X	X	X	X	X	$6,
									$45,080

Contrarian Marketing Process (1 of 3)

Enriching Your Customer Information

Pattern Analysis

Pattern Analysis

Start with your Customer & Transaction Information

Segment & Enrich Customer Data by . . .

Segment & Enrich Customer Data

Append RFM (Recency, Frequency, Monetary) Information

Enrich Customer Data with SIC (Industry) codes, # employees, company size, etc.

Understand Your Strengths

% Revenue & Profits Generated by Top 5% & 10% of Customers
Average $ Transaction Value
Lifetime $ Value
Concentrations by SIC, # employees, company size, etc.

Customer Segmentation (6)
• Best-of-the-Best (B-of-B)
• Future B-of-B
• New
• Recently Departed
• Long Lost
• Testers

Profile Analysis

1. Top 5% Customers: % Revenue & Profits

2. Top 10% Customers: % Revenue & Profits

Operationalize: Integrate into Business Plan

Tie Your Company's Financial Plan to Your Customer Goals to Determine How Many Customers You Need

---

1. Quantify # of B-of-B Customers Currently Have & Goal for Future

2. Quantify # of B-of-B Prospects You Need & Goal

Design Marketing Budget Process to Support B-of-B (19, pg 165)

Activity Generation

1. Make a List of Top B-of-B Customers

2. Clone B-of-B & Future B-of-B Customers to Prospects

3. Make a List of Target Names for Prospective Customers

Contrarian Marketing Process (2 of 3)

Implementation

Create the B-of-B Customer Experience and Integrate into Touch Points by Department

Sales & Marketing Campaign Activation

Marketing & Sales Preparation

Create B-of-B Marketing Calendar that Identifies Key Activities by Customer by Week & Month

Review Tools of the Trade: Technology, Processes & Measurement

5 Alarm Fire: Develop Early Warning System for Recently Departed Customers

Managing Sales People the Mavrick Way

Marketing & Sales Agree on Campaign Structure

Create & Manage Sales Pipeline for B-of-B Customers & Prospects

Contrarian Marketing Success Focused on B-of-B Customers and Prospects

Implementation Continued, Contrarian Marketing Process (3 of 3)

Implementation

Analyze the Customer Experience

Review Customer Experience Touch Points

Pre-Purchase

Awareness	Contact
Reputation & Word of Mouth Picking customers before they pick us Advertising & Public Relations Web-site Events Philanthropic Initiatives	Information inquiry through: • Sales visit • Web-site • Phone call • Mail, E-mail • Visit to store

Purchase

Purchase	Delivery
Ease of contact Flexibility Shows interest and listens* Ability to match commercial offer to customer needs Industry expertise Sales material Proactive in replying Follow up	Regular delivery of information Delivery on-time Delivered with quality Delivery person Training Follow up after delivery

Post-Purchase

Product Usage	Service & Parts	Customer Complaints	Customer Relations
Received as New & up-to-date Performance, uptime and productivity Follow up	Service availability and quality Overall service expertise and passion Follow up	Submit complaint Feedback/ Update Response time Complaint resolution Complaint closing Follow Up	Personal communication: • Phone call • Mail, E-mail • Customer visit Marketing material: • Brochure • Product catalog • Sales flyers, etc. Customer Events • Philanthropic • Initiatives

Contrarian Marketing Turotial (1 of 2)

Marketing Bill of Rights

Avoiding 4 Basic Traps

Apply Best Practices

1. Marketing Success Can Be Engineered by Mathematically Tying Business & Financial Objectives to Retention & Acquisition of B-of-B Customers

2. Use a Bottom-Up Approach to Craft Your Marketing Strategy

3. Marketing tactics for your best customers and prospects can be identified and agreed upon with your field offices and sales teams.

4. A data-centric approach to marketing sets the strategy for field offices and sales teams, and is used to allocate the budget to each.

---

1. The Ego Trap
2. The Competition Trap
3. The Messaging Trap
4. The Customer Trap

---

1. Marketing is 90% Mathematical, 10% Creative

2. Sustaining marketing campaigns on predictable time-frames allows customers to expect information consistently, and often, is more important than getting it right once.

3. Stick to the basics. Ideally, focus on one primary message.

4. Understand the Concept of Cost per Impression to evaluate marketing investments.

5. Understand the Concept of 'Cost per Qualified Lead.

6. Be Contrarian Where You Spend Your Marketing Funds. Evaluate Your Competitors and Focus Where Your Competitors Do Not Focus (4, 18).

7. Decide whether your company wants to be all things to all people.

8. Align your marketing initiatives directly with your sales initiatives by sharing a specific list of target customers and prospects with your sales team.

9. Align your marketing messaging with the customer experience that your operation delivers.

10. Focus only on a few 'Best of the Best' customers and prospects so you can pick your customers and prospects before they pick you.

11. Understand Branding: Promise vs. Expectation

Contrarian Marketing Turotial (2 of 2)

Activating Your Contrarian Marketing Strategy

Focus on Top 5% & 10% of Customers that Generate > 70% of Revenue & Profits.

Spoiling the B-of-B.

Establish Your Marketing Strategy for Next B-of-B customers.

Build the Marketing Calendar, Customer Model & Budget.

Managing Salespeople the Mavrick Way.

Giving Back:

Will you join us in giving back? One hundred percent of all profits generated by Contrarian Marketing books and DVDs are donated to our favorite organization, the Folds of Honor Foundation.

Folds of Honor provides post-secondary educational scholarships to the spouses and children of service members disabled or killed as a result of their military service to our great nation.

Today's servicemen and women bear the incredible burden of combat and face the same economic strain faced by the rest of the country. Folds of Honor recognizes the federal government's work to support its military service families, but it cannot succeed alone without proactive civilian organizations to assist.

Photo courtesy of Volvo Rents.

ALL GAVE SOME.
SOME GAVE ALL.
NOW IT'S OUR
TURN TO GIVE.

To learn more about the Folds of Honor Foundation, visit www.foldsofhonor.org.

Made in the USA
Charleston, SC
21 January 2012